Hurly Brogan

D0419551

HOUSE OF ILL FAME

HOUSE OF ILL FAME

Simon Hoggart

Illustrated by John Jensen

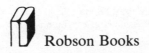 Robson Books

The author and publishers would like to thank the editor and proprietors of *Punch* magazine for permission to reproduce material in this book. Thanks are also owed to the editor and proprietors of the *Observer* for permission to reproduce additional material.

First published in Great Britain in 1985 by Robson Books Ltd., Bolsover House, 5–6 Clipstone Street, London W1P 7EB. Text copyright © 1985 Simon Hoggart, illustrations copyright © 1985 John Jensen

British Library Cataloguing in Publication Data

Hoggart, Simon
  House of ill fame: a selection from Punch's
  On the House column.
  I. Title II. Punch
  828'.91407   PN6175

ISBN 0 86051 350 5

Typeset by Spire Print Services Ltd., Salisbury
Printed in Great Britain by St Edmundsbury Press, Bury St Edmunds

Introduction

When I first went to work at the House of Commons in 1973, the *Guardian* sketchwriter was Norman Shrapnel. A dignified, laconic man, he wrote a daily report of the proceedings in the chamber. It was elegant and stylish, and usually demonstrated Norman's gift for extending a single metaphor until you thought it would snap, but never quite did. Most parliamentary reporting is office gossip about the most influential office in the country, and MPs used to love the Shrapnel column. They found it difficult, however, to meet Shrapnel.

Now and again they would get a sighting. A colleague on the *Guardian* might introduce him, after which Norman would remain in the conversation for as short a time as he could without appearing rude, and then silently disappear. After work he preferred to drink in the press bar, where few MPs ever penetrate.

I once asked him why he spent so much time avoiding the people he wrote about. 'If I got to know them,' he said glumly, 'it might spoil the purity of my hatred.'

I could see his point without really agreeing with it. MPs are not for the most part fit objects of loathing. Indeed, they always seem to me to reflect closely the make-up of humanity at large – the vain, the stupid, the agreeable, the intelligent, the garrulous and the taciturn, the shy and the extrovert, the malicious and the kind-hearted, and so forth. That's not to say that they are a market researcher's cross section of society: women are badly under-represented, lawyers and teachers wildly over-provided. But the character of the bare,

5

forked animal is there, laid out for all to see. I suspect that people who say they detest all politicians are afraid of the politician in themselves.

One side of the typical MP's character which is perhaps more attractive than one might suppose is that they can take criticism and jokes at their own expense. This is not, of course, an invariable rule. I related in *Punch* a story about Mr Cranley Onslow, now the Chairman of the 1922 Committee, which caused him such offence that he suggested I ought to resign my membership of the Commons Press Gallery as a matter of honour. I declined to do so on the grounds that journalists are under no duty to be polite about MPs. A quick glance through the files revealed that Mr Onslow had in the past been strikingly rude about many of his fellow members. But this was not altogether surprising: it is often the ones who dish it out most eagerly who dislike getting it back.

But the majority of MPs take it very well, and even enjoy it, as, somewhat to their chagrin, the makers of 'Spitting Image' discovered. Frank Johnson of *The Times* who, with Michael White of the *Guardian,* was one of the two funniest sketchwriters of the acerbic modern school, used to dread mingling with MPs, especially those he had insulted in print. When White persuaded him that they actually wished to meet him in order to compliment him, he summoned up his courage and chatted to several, who promptly lionized him. Those to whom he had been most offensive would ask: 'And shall we be *enjoying* you again in the morning?'

Personally I am always struck by the manner in which politicians like to mythologize themselves, preferring even an unpleasant mask to tedious workaday reality. Mr Norman Tebbit is a far kindlier man than he cares to make out. Eric Heffer is, I fear, a trifle vain, but he is also genial and even tender-hearted – quite unlike the snarling brute who lowers at the TV cameras. Mr Steel is more ruthless than he cares to have generally known, Mr Denis Healey less so. Often I suspect that the image they acquire for themselves acts as a shield from the outside world. An actor playing the villain

6

does not mind being jeered; he would find it intolerable if the audience were booing at *him*.

I make few claims for these small anecdotes and observations except that, once or twice, they might enable the reader to peer behind the mask and glimpse the person hiding there.

SIMON HOGGART

June 1985

Mrs Thatcher
in a
morale-boosting
pin-up pose.

MRS THATCHER'S morning generally begins the previous night. One of the ministers describes a typical encounter. 'It's 1 am and you've had a hell of a day, so you're tottering down a Commons corridor with a whole bottle of claret swilling around inside you wondering when on earth you can go to bed, when you see this vision in blue drifting along looking as if she's just emerged from the beauty parlour. "Ah," she says, "how are you, dear? Now tell me what you think about these new statistics! And *what* do you propose to do about them?" It is absolutely terrifying.'

Sometimes she is weaving her way around the late-night committees bolstering the morale of her troops, like Henry V on St Crispin's Eve. With her is her devoted parliamentary private secretary, and as she roams the corridors he whispers in her ear, telling her who is of the True Faith and who has been heard to take her name in vain over buttered crumpets in the tea room. Then the Rover sweeps her back to Downing Street, where there is just time to squeeze in another hour's work on the Red Boxes, those urgent governmental papers on which every prime minister must spend hours of each day.

Or rather, on which this prime minister spends hours every day. Probably no premier in history has devoted so long to the boxes. She is the living refutation of Parkinson's Law, proof that time expands to accommodate the work available for it. She is obsessively industrious, a source of much resentment to those who work with her. 'I regard it as quite unwholesome,' another minister says.

At 2 am or even later, she is in the flat at the top of Downing Street, tucked up in her bed. She dislikes going to bed because it means she has to stop work. She might read a page or two of a book: Kipling, perhaps, of whose writing she can quote great chunks by heart. Or it might be an Improving Work by a right-wing thinker. 'If she sees a thought she likes, such as "You cannot abolish proverty by first abolishing wealth," she will underline it twice and show it to you,' according to one MP.

She is not between the sheets for long. Whenever she went to bed, she will be up around 6.30 or even earlier; startled staff have sometimes been asked if they heard an item on 'Farming Today', which begins at 6.10). Leaving Denis to sleep, she makes her own breakfast of toast or grapefruit while she listens to the BBC 'Today' programme. Downing Street is really London's most elegant office block, and downstairs the staff are beginning to clock in.

From 8 to 9 she will finish off the last of the night's boxes. 'She thinks that she must know everything that is going on, every single detail,' a cabinet minister says. 'It can be infuriating. She just will not allow you to get on with it.' She might spare a moment to glance through the newspapers, but certainly no longer. She flips through the pop papers as well as the heavy ones, and will give as much weight to a headline in the *Sun* as to a pundit's paragraph in *The Times* or the *Guardian*. She hardly ever reads articles about herself, and she never watches herself on television. Every day a digest of the press is prepared for her, and this is brief, even curt. For example: 'The Energy Secretary's speech is widely reported. It is being interpreted as an attack on your economic policy.'

Meetings begin at 9 o'clock, and on Tuesdays and Thursdays the first session is devoted to plotting Prime Minister's Questions. This 15-minute session is regarded as of crucial importance, partly because she permits any topic at all to be raised.

'She thinks that Questions are her hot-line to the British people,' a close associate says. 'She believes there is this

10

terrible great weight of bureaucracy and government on top of everyone, so she has to appeal over their heads.

'She's the woman under the dryer chatting to her friends, and there they are on about the judge who gave a short sentence to a rapist. She says "Tut, tut, isn't it shocking, if I was Prime Minister I'd do something about it," and a fairy godmother turns up and says "But you *are* Prime Minister and you can do something about it!" So that poor judge got his awful public wigging.'

'Her upbringing as a grocer's daughter is absolutely central to her outlook,' says a minister who knows her well. 'Her belief in sound money has got nothing to do with hi-falutin' Chicago economists. She just knows that you cannot spend more than you take in at the till. She often refers to her father's shop as if it had lessons for running an industrialized economy. I would bet she has never been in debt in her life.'

She has always preferred to make up her own mind without troubling her colleagues for their views. Her notorious 'swamping' remark on immigration came from the top of her head during a TV interview. Willie Whitelaw, who had to build a policy around the phrase, first heard of it from the Press Association tapes. She often likes to give the impression that her ministers are actually nothing to do with her. 'You half expect her to say "If you ask me, I blame the government," ' an MP says. 'I remember one session in the tea room when she was hammering on about the nationalized industries, and how disgraceful they were, putting up prices and so on, as if she had no part in it at all. We sat there with our jaws hanging open, but nobody dared to say anything.'

She loves a good argument and will shout 'That's absolute nonsense, don't be so wet' at someone. This angers quite a few people, and they hint darkly that she will one day pay for her disloyalty. Her admirers claim it is her way of testing the strength of her own case, a dress rehearsal for the arguments she will face later. 'Politics isn't a Hinge and Brackett tea party, it's the real world, and it's tough,' one of them says.

Probably without knowing it, she can make people's

brains freeze. 'I was in Downing Street with a cabinet minister she got on well with, and during the discussion she made two important factual errors,' an MP recalls. 'Nobody, including the senior minister, corrected her. I suddenly realized he was afraid.' Worse than her occasional shouts and crisp put-downs is the way she can look at people. 'I'd made some bad mistake which caused her a lot of trouble,' one of her staff says. 'I expected a real dressing-down. Instead she gave me this *look* which meant: "Nanny is not cross. She is just very, very sad." It was ghastly.'

Whisked between official residences in official cars, prime ministers soon become sealed off from the real world and begin to place exaggerated store by their meetings with ordinary people, whether across a factory bench or a gin and tonic. But nobody, introduced to the Prime Minister, is going to start by attacking her. Reality soon begins to disappear, like a shape half-glimpsed in the mist, discerned only through short, haphazard and misleading encounters. Which is more real, which (if any) tells you more about the British people: a girl in a chocolate factory, mumbling politely into the fondants; Jimmy Savile, paying one of his frequent visits to talk about Stoke Mandeville hospital, or a crowd of yelling demonstrators? 'You see, they all go mad, they all start hearing voices,' says an MP who has studied several prime ministers.

If she has no official dinner she will return to the Commons to chat to Conservative MPs. Sometimes she will take a quick snack in the cafeteria, the only prime minister to make a habit of this. She invariably has buck rarebit, toasted cheese with an egg on top. Sometimes she decides to eat in the members' dining room, in which case her parliamentary private secretary is sent before her, to prepare The Way.

As she arrives the gossip and the small talk, the rumble of half-sozzled conversation is suddenly silenced. She distributes quick and searching questions about the state of the economy or the world. Eager sycophants praise her last speech, her dazzling parliamentary barbs. Members who had

12

hoped to order another bottle of House of Commons red think better of it. Those who were about to leave remain glued to their green leather chairs. 'You can tell her mood from her clothes,' one says. 'Shimmery in blue means she's confident, on top of things. Red, speckly clothes mean she has problems, she's fussed.'

Sometimes someone will get it horribly wrong. 'Robin Maxwell-Hyslop had done something to please her, and when she sat down she said: "Ah, dear Robin!" So, emboldened, he launched into a long and risqué anecdote he'd read in *Private Eye*. Nothing could stop him. He went on and on. She sat there, frozen and po-faced. It was awful, unimaginable.'

Apart from occasional visits to the opera (when she has usually read the libretto beforehand) her own family are her only real interest outside politics. In particular, she worries about Mark who, it must be said, is far from loved by his mother's circle of acquaintance. 'She was only ever in a bad mood when he failed his accountancy exams,' a former colleague says, 'so that was pretty often.' The one time she has cracked in Downing Street was when he seemed lost in the Sahara.

'The point about Denis is that he is exactly like the *Private Eye* letters,' says a friend. He himself hates them, and particularly the stage show *Anyone for Denis* because they depict him as an incompetent ninny and, as he often points out, he was the managing director of a large firm. He is also very rich.

But the social style: the drinks, golf in the Algarve with Bill Deedes, editor of the *Daily Telegraph*, the vocabulary, the attitudes—all these are pure 'Dear Bill.' He does have strong views about the Bolshies who run the unions, he does say 'just time for a tincture,' he does call her 'the Boss' and he firmly believes that the BBC is run by a crowd of pinkoes.

Some people think that he is in awe of her, but it seems more likely that he has simply learned to live with the bossiness of the average self-assured British middle-class woman. A friend tells the story of a Downing Street reception where

13

Denis was drinking gin and tonic. A Special Branch detective hove up and whispered in his ear: 'The Boss is back, sir,' As Denis's left hand poured the gin into a convenient pot plant, his right arm stretched out to greet his wife.

'He is marvellous when she's down,' says someone who knows them both well. 'He's a great backslapper and very encouraging. But I think he is more worrying when she's up. He sweeps her along, and reinforces her instinct when a little caution would help.'

She is not at her ease in the royal presence. One insider tells the story of an annual prime ministerial visit to Balmoral. The Royal Family usually has a barbeque on the estate, lighting their own fire, grilling their own sausages, and so forth. 'She was terribly agitato, and can you blame her? All those Hanoverians on horseback. Afterwards the Queen insisted on washing up, in a little hut. Margaret was appalled and wanted to do it herself, but the Queen wouldn't let her, because it was the one day of the year she can pretend to be a real person.' One is left with this vivid image of Britain's two leading women locked in genteel combat over the Fairy Liquid.

She doesn't really have friends in the sense that most people do, because friends imply leisure, which she doesn't believe in. But she sees people she admires and who can help her: Sir Hector Laing, the chairman of United Biscuits; Lord (Hugh) Thomas, the right-wing historian, is particularly esteemed; Ronnie Millar, a playwright who has written more forgotten dramas than Ernie Wise, helps with her speeches—he coined the phrase 'The lady's not for turning.' She likes men who treat her with a certain insouciant gallantry. 'It's a kind of hearty pink ginnery,' a friend says. 'People who say "Margaret, you're looking perfectly splendid!" She loves it, and not many men dare try it. Humphrey Atkins did. So does Robin Leigh-Pemberton. So does Marcus Sieff. In a platonic way, of course, she fancies them.'

Few gain access to the innermost sanctum, the sitting room in the flat above Downing Street. One is Norman Tebbit, formerly Employment Secretary, since head of Trade and Industry, probably the man she most admires in her cabinet. 'Basically she thinks that everyone is useless except Norman' says a backbencher who knows her well.

But if she wishes that everybody could be like Tebbit there is one man to whom, above everyone else, she has cause to be grateful. Willie Whitelaw was sorry not to have beaten her for the party leadership in 1976, but it was largely his own fault, since his code of loyalty would not allow him to stand against Ted Heath. The day after she won he told her: 'I am now your most loyal supporter,' but it was six months or so before she took him into her confidence.

In spite of swearing fealty, he entertained the gravest doubts from the beginning. He once bellowed at a friend: 'That woman thinks she has a hot-line to the British people. She hasn't!' But when she won the 1979 election, he was one of the first two people into Downing Street (the other was Humphrey Atkins) to help form the new cabinet. She is, contrary to general belief, rather scatter-brained, and had not drafted a cabinet beforehand, giving as her excuse the fact that it might not be needed. 'Apart from the top jobs and the fact that there was nothing for Ted Heath, she had no idea of what she wanted,' a staff member reports. 'And that's one reason why her cabinet was so weighted towards the wets at first. Willie, and later Peter Carrington, wrote in a lot of the names for her.'

Jim Prior's despatch to the distant shores of Ulster was her most cunning piece of hatchet work; he had said publicly that he did not want the job, and friends such as Carrington and Walker had urged him not to take it. But her cajolery and wheedling ('I know you will do it so well, I've had it in mind for you for *such* a long time'), combined with Prior's fear of seeming cowardly, persuaded him to take it. Her triumph was complete. 'The Falklands brought her the support of the voters, but she had beaten the Tory establishment the year before,' an admirer says.

I asked one of her Chosen Few whether, as she finally turns out the light in the Downing Street bedroom, she might ever be troubled by the fear that she had got it all

15

wrong that, far from saving Britain, she might be wrecking it. He thought for a moment, then shook his head. 'You see, we believed very strongly that we are actually right and that we have to keep on going. We cannot afford to indulge in needless self-doubt. Some politicians doubt themselves and they fall into vacillation. She will never do that.'

In 1982 Cecil Parkinson was an exotic figure, scarcely known to the general public.

CECIL PARKINSON, then Chairman of the Conservative Party, was a man of whom we knew little until the Falklands crisis hurled him, like General Galtieri, Brian Hanrahan and the Upland Goose Hotel, out of his previous anonymity. I heard, however, a very curious tale about him.

He was addressing a meeting of mill-owners and other prosperous businessmen in Lancashire, the country of his birth. He expatiated warmly on the area, how splendid its architecture, how familiar each corner and pathway, how delightful its people. 'I know it so well, that I even had my first orgasm here!' he told the startled industrialists.

In 1982 Tony Benn eagerly supported the railwaymen's strike.

'IN THE WORLD I live in,' Tony Benn has said, 'nobody ever feels that their view has been fairly represented.' Ah, the world Tony Benn lives in! What a fabulous, in the literal sense of that overworked word, place it must be. Like Oz or Erewhon, it may not exist but is nonetheless vivid, colourful and even more real than the sub-fusc, quotidian world the rest of us inhabit.

Now and again we may get glimpses of Benn's world,

16

Cecil Parkinson
in
TRUE GRIT

Wilderness

usually a brief flash, but as indelibly printed on the mind as Xanadu before the person from Porlock arrived.

Benn was attending a meeting in the House of Commons along with Ray Buckton and various left-wing MPs who supported the Aslef strike. They discussed strategy and tactics, and how public opinion might be influenced in favour of Aslef. Then Benn said that in his view they should 'capitalize on support for the strike among commuters'. He suggested that collecting boxes, possibly marked 'Save the Trains', ought to be placed at terminals, so that travellers might be able to show their real feelings about the strike, unlike the lying anti-strike propaganda printed in the newspapers.

This, I sometimes think, is the charm of Tony Benn. Like many great writers, Frances Hodgson Burnett and J. R. Tolkien, for example, he offers a delightful and comforting fantasy world into which all his admirers can escape.

There was a brief ruction concerning the travel expenses charged by members of the European Parliament.

I WAS DELIGHTED to find that in the midst of the scandal of the European Parliament expenses some MEPs complained that they weren't getting enough. Winnie Ewing, who sits in the interest of the people of northern Scotland, pointed out that she has to travel around a constituency the size of Denmark. She loses some £3,000 a year of her own money. Others are less self-abnegating. It has been estimated that, by claiming the full permitted amount, a Greek MEP can make a profit of £342 every time he travels from Athens.

The figure from London to Strasbourg is a piddling £92 a trip, barely enough to buy one decent meal in the city. Germans can do exceedingly well: all their MEPs have free travel on the national railways. So they can, if they are so disposed, take a ride to the border followed by a bus trip costing coppers into Alsace, thus making a gigantic profit every time they arrive for their legislative duties.

MPs SPEND A LOT OF TIME swapping canvassing stories. Simon Mahon, the former MP for Bootle, told me this one. Another member had been doing the rounds of his constituency. As he walked up one garden path, a large and friendly dog bounded down to meet him. He knocked on the door, and when it was opened, the dog rushed inside. The residents turned out to be Labour supporters and were delighted to offer their MP a cup of tea, which he accepted gratefully, since it had been a long and tiring day.

As they sat round the coffee table making polite conversation, the dog suddenly cocked its leg and peed on the floor. To the MP's even greater surprise, the people who were giving him tea said nothing about it; indeed carried on as if nothing whatever had happened.

Very shortly after this curious moment he rose to go, thanking his host and hostess for their kindness, hoping that they would not forget to vote on election day. As he reached the door, they asked politely: 'Aren't you going to take your dog with you?'

ANOTHER GOOD ONE comes from Delwyn Williams, the Tory MP for Montgomery who was going down a street tucking his leaflet into people's letter-boxes when he noticed that the Labour workers had got there first. So before he put his own pamphlet through the slit, he privily took theirs out, quickly amassing a small collection.

As he walked through one garden it struck him as surprisingly muddy, so he looked around and saw to his horror that he had left a trail of footprints up a freshly cemented path. The thing was an almost irreparable mess. So he quickly

19

tucked a single, Labour, leaflet into the door, and tiptoed away again.

THE MOST FAMOUS POLITICAL CORRESPONDENT in Britain has been featured in the *Tatler*, the guide to all social success. Indubitably the hardest working of all lobby correspondents is Christopher Moncrieff, of the Press Association. Mr Moncrieff frequently works a twenty-hour day, at one time pausing only to refresh himself with the occasional glass of draught Guinness, though he is now teetotal.

He is not, however, a particularly snappy dresser. Indeed Michael Foot is Yves St Laurent by comparison. At a press briefing given by General Haig in Washington Moncrieff asked a pertinent and difficult question. Haig didn't even try to answer. He glared at Moncrieff, then said: '*Where* did you get those trousers?'

'In a trouser shop,' Moncrieff replied, rather wittily I thought.

A week or so later he was the one British reporter allowed into the working breakfast at Downing Street for the Prime Minister, Haig, President Reagan and Francis Pym. This does not actually mean that the correspondent scoffs any of the kidneys and kedgeree; instead he is allowed in for two minutes solely to record the scene. Moncrieff, who simply never stops working, kept asking questions of the President, who did not merely decline to answer them, but behaved as if he could not even hear them—a difficult feat when someone is bellowing at you from five yards.

Later, Moncrieff muttered that Reagen 'must be deaf or something', a remark which, surprisingly, appeared in the *White House Pooled Report*, a journal which circulates among political correspondents in Washington. In a puzzled description of the British hacks, it claimed that Moncrieff had replied to Haig: 'In a pants shope, you fool,' a form of words I cannot conceive so courteous a man would use.

THE RELATIONSHIP of politicians with the press has always been fascinating. How strange it must feel to be prime minister and to know that your name will probably appear in every single national newspaper every single day, and that you will be vilified frequently, sometimes in print, sometimes by harsh caricature.

Some have egos so enormous that they can survive anything. As well try to fell a rhinoceros with an air pistol. Others hate it. I remember Michael Heseltine asking himself how he managed to face his own children, knowing they had read in the papers what he had also read about himself.

Many of them are obsessed by the press and what it says. People like Harold Wilson and Denis Healey, when in office, would read everything about themselves and their works which they could lay their hands on. They would scrutinize an article by, for instance, David Watt, then on the *Financial Times*, and if the very last paragraph contained something they did not like, they would become upset, and even seek out Mr Watt to complain. This in spite of the fact those few lines might have been seen by one member of the population in a thousand.

I even recall myself being admonished by James Callaghan, or at least by his press secretary, for having reported, in the dark and obscure undergrowth of a *Guardian* inside page, that the Prime Minister had winked in a meaningful manner. He might have winked, the press secretary conceded, but the downward movement of the eyelid had been involuntary and had no political significance.

In my experience it is generally the best politicians who take their medicine like soldiers. The complaints are most likely to come from the forgotten and the also-rans, whose rankling sense of failure makes them most vulnerable to the taunts of the media.

Recently I had a fascinating chat on this very subject with someone who knows Mrs Thatcher well and has often watched her at work. He tells me, and I have no reason whatever to doubt him, that she pays only scant attention to

21

what appears in the papers, and is particularly loath to read articles about herself.

Hand her a feature titled: 'Maggie's Brilliant Success' and she may peruse it for a very few seconds before tossing it aside. Give her a clipping: 'Why Thatcher Must Resign Now–by the Editor of *The Times*' and she will not even look at it.

What she does do is glance at the headlines, in order to get a broad and general feel for what the press is saying. And she will attach as much weight to the two-inch lettering of the blotchy *Sun* as to the more restrained and orotund headlines of the posh papers.

This, I gather, had some effect on her handling of the Falklands crisis. The carefully pondered and intricately argued leading articles in the heavyweight prints were unread and ignored, while the strident cries of the *Sun* and the *Star* ('Up Yours Galtieri', and 'No Sell-Out To The Argies') helped to keep her resolution firm during those long, anxious, and, we have since learned, half-starved, night-time lucubrations.

Most people came to regard the much-vaunted Register of Members' Interests as a sour joke.

SOME YEARS AGO I was charged with the task of writing about the Totalisator Bill, a doomed piece of legislation which would have allowed the Tote to set up betting shops. I discovered that the principal reason for the bill's failure was the determined and effective animosity of Brian Walden, now a popular television interviewer, then the Labour MP for Birmingham, Ladywood. Mr Walden had been paid a

22

sum of money by the Bookmakers' Association, and while he had referred glancingly to this fact, he had kept mute about all the important details. He was paid a total of £25,000 a year by various organizations.

This astounding quantity of boodle, the equivalent of more than £100,000 today, caused some ripples at the time and was one of a number of events leading to the formation of the Register of Members' Interests. This document is roughly as useful to the seeker after truth as the old White Star Line timetable would be to a modern transatlantic traveller.

Indeed James Fenton once suggested that it should be replaced by a Register of Members' Sexual Interests, which would be simultaneously much more interesting and more informative. He got scant co-operation from MPs in this endeavour, though one Tory knight did claim that he was fond of 'hedgehogs–tightly curled hedgehogs. They present such a challenge'.

For a start few MPs are as proud of their crocks of lucre as Mr Walden. Many are positively laconic, even silent. Enoch Powell and his deadly enemy the Rev Ian Paisley simply refused to fill in the form. When we disobey the laws parliament creates, we get fined or go to prison, yet when MPs do the same, nothing whatever happens to them. Others create the same effect by writing 'nil' in the space provided. I name no names, but some of these people seem to live rather well on an MP's salary. Perhaps they are just economical, persuading their wives to use margarine and walking to the next fare stage to save money on the buses.

Some are prissily exact about every fiver earned from the BBC, every free trip to visit a nickel plating mill, each penny coughed up by their union for election expenses. Others have directorships in firms which, while again I may not give names, appear to have more to do with shifting blocks of money from one rich man's pocket to another's than with increasing the nation's wealth. Some are magnificently vague. Michael Jopling 'has an interest in land and property'. Geoffery Finsberg, likewise, has 'an interest in a few

23

rented properties'. How many is a 'few'? And are they small terraced cottages, or do they include Centre Point? We are left to surmise.

Mrs Thatcher lists 'nil', though it would be fascinating to read Denis's entry, were he called on to provide one. Michael Foot gets 'royalties from time to time . . .' and nothing else. Tony Benn is remarkably precise about how his election expenses are paid; he spends six lines of the register describing the process. Under shareholdings, however, he lists only the family firm Benn Brothers Ltd. This is not terribly helpful, since it does not tell us how many shares he owns, and when I last looked the company was worth just over seven million pounds.

The problem is that the terms under which the register operates are far too vague and permit far too many loopholes to be of any real use to us at all. Nobody is going to write: 'Free trip to visit torture cells in Chile, interests in international armaments and child chimney-sweeps' agency, numerous East End sweat shops and eighty hovels (twenty-seven evictions last year).' If the terms were tightened up to extract honesty from all MPs, they wouldn't vote for the register in the first place. Naturally they have a long farrago of excuses for not telling us, the voters, what their real interests are, so I don't suppose for a moment that we will ever know. In the meantime, the wretched register might as well be scrapped.

Let us not forget that, before Ken Livingstone and his friends became popular national heroes, they were cordially disliked.

I HAVE NOTICED a startling and, I think, rather disturbing trend in British politics–the use of children as campaign props. Of course, MPs are forever wittering on about children (though I have never seen one kiss a baby, and I once watched Ted Heath refuse to do so) as if the mere fact of possessing progeny gave them a claim on the voters' affections. At the Gower by-election the Labour candidate made a point of discussing rusks, rattles and Bonjela with any young mother he met. But his Tory opponent went further with the Politics Of Pampers by actually bringing his nine-month old daughter to his press conferences, where she alternately played with her toys and cried.

If the candidate's wife had been out at work, or if the family were thrown out of their boarding house at 8.30 in the morning, there might have been some excuse. But their home was only two miles away, and there can have been no motive except the peculiar belief that people are more likely to vote for someone who has proved himself fertile than someone who hasn't.

Rather more worrying than this, however, is an article in the *Guardian* by Frances Morrell, who is deputy leader of the Inner London Education Authority and a member of the GLC. She used to be Tony Benn's political adviser. She has been sending an official GLC car to pick up her children from school, a prima facie abuse of her position which she and two of her colleagues firmly defend. 'We wish to state immediately and unequivocally that we ... use official transport in this way, and as mothers, have no alternative.'

She goes on to say that if transport at the ratepayers' expense were not available, then no mother who lacked the cash for a second car or a nanny could enter public life. These cars make it possible for working people and members of ethnic minorities to 'serve'.

This article provides a remarkably revealing insight into the minds of politicians– politicians of any sex, hue or credo. Take that splendid weasel word 'serve', always used by pols to describe their own occupation. It is a part of the old conjugation: 'I serve, you get elected, he is hungry for power.' It's worth repeating that politicians stand for public office because they want to, not because they have a longing to help their fellows.

Then there is the dazzling ability possessed by pols, both left and right, to justify philosophically whatever it is they want to do, whether cutting taxes, visiting Afghanistan or getting their children brought home in limousines. Ms Morrell doesn't merely say that having the kids picked up is an agreeable perk, like a company credit card or free coal for miners. She claims that it is a necessary condition of socialism, feminism and freedom.

There are two answers to Ms Morrell, both of which will have occurred already to readers, but which do not seemed to have crossed her mind.

First, one might ask why she imagines that her chosen job, which is politics, gives her a greater right to transport at public expense than a mother who happens to be a doctor, a barrister or an office cleaner?

Secondly, I find it hard to believe that she or her children are so unpopular and friendless that there is no other parent at the school who will arrange to give them a lift home every day. Hundreds of thousands of children whose mothers work are brought home in this way every day of the school year.

There are more interesting points in this whole wretched business. There is the fact that, because Ms Morrell has convinced herself that what she is doing is all right, it does not occur to her that ordinary voters might not agree. Like many politicians, she has finally lost touch with reality.

I later spoke to Jack Straw, a former colleague of Ms Morrell's and learned that in her days as a functionary of the National Union of Students Ms Morrell was notorious for using taxis for any purpose that came to mind, and putting the fares onto her bulging expense claims. So celebrated was she that once, when out with Jack Straw she hailed a cab. He saw a bus going exactly in their direction. 'Just for once, Frances,' he pleaded, 'couldn't we take this big red taxi instead?'

ROY JENKINS was fortunate enough to arrive late for his important speech to the 1982 Liberal Assembly.

26

Some of the stranger manifestations of the Liberal soul might have made him ponder whether an alliance with these people was really such a good idea after all.

For example, there was the heavy aroma of the chairman's announcement shortly before his speech: 'Would Lord Avebury please go to the "Liberator" stall to collect his Uruguay leaflets.'

Moments later, in the debate on South America, a man quite seriously called for a massive effort to send second-hand typewriters to Liberal parties in reactionary Latin American countries.

One had a ghostly vision of similar earnest young men sitting in the steaming jungle clearings of the Amazon tapping out press releases on site value rating and ramblers' rights.

Earlier Mr Jenkins also missed the debate on animal welfare. Another young man, who was wildly applauded by a large section of the audience, declared: 'As Liberals, we should fight against speciesism just as we fight racism and sexism!'

At that point the mind begins to spin gently out of control. Do they mean that animals should have full voting rights, British citizenship and council creches? And are not many animals, such as wolverines and sharks, guilty of speciesism themselves, by eating their comrades in the struggle against oppression?

There might also be conflicts between the various 'isms' which Liberals are obliged to follow. It must be speciesist to call someone a 'male chauvinist pig'.

Finally Mr Jenkins made it to the platform. He was at his smoothest, most glutinous best. It was like being drowned in a vat of molten nougat.

He contrived to give the Liberals credit for the foundation of the SDP–specifically Jo Grimond, from whom stemmed 'the whole idea of a realignment of politics'.

At that, the silvery old statesman, who nowadays devotes the twilight of his years to stirring and generally making trouble, beamed pinkly with pleasure.

27

I ADORE THE ROWS between the various swivel-eyed sects on the fringe of the big parties. There was a beauty between the Workers Revolutionary Party, which is Vanessa Redgrave's lot, and the paper *Socialist Organiser.*

It's worth remembering, by the way, that the far left suffers from the exact opposite of paranoia; instead they have the insane delusion that they are followed by millions of ordinary workers who support them and wish them well, a belief untouched by their constant humiliating electoral failures. I would like to reprint all of the WRP's reply to *Socialist Organiser* but two sample sentences will have to stand for the rest. They provide a whiff of the whole gamy feud.

'The substance of the defamatory statements complained of [the WRP writes] should be repeated so that the labour movement is informed of their gravity. Mr Matgamna [of *Socialist Organiser* fame] said that: "The Workers Revolutionary Party is a 'pseudo-Marxist gobbledegook-spouting cross between the Moonies, the Scientologists and the Jones Cult which committed mass suicide in the Guyana jungle three years ago." '

I think that if someone said that about me I might very well sue, but I rather doubt that I would have the nerve to reprint it.

THE 1982 TORY PARTY conference was distinguished, as ever, by the perfervid nature of its resolutions. Some 889 were sent in though of course only a handful were actually debated. Everyone's favourite was as usual, from the Law & Order section. It was from Norwood Conservatives and read: 'This Conference calls upon the Government to recreate the conditions in which a virgin leading a child and carrying a bag of gold could pass on foot from one end of the Kingdom to another without fear.'

Leaving aside the obvious questions, such as what a virgin is doing with a child in the first place (perhaps she is a pram-snatcher, another example of increasing lawlessness), why she is carrying a bag of gold at all when it could be in the bank and why, if she possesses an entire bag, she doesn't spend some of it on a train ticket, we are left to ponder the word 'recreate'.

Was there ever a time when virgins could get beyond Polperro without having their gold snatched? And if so when was it? For the whole of our history there have been parts of the Kingdom where no-one, not even a harlot with a bag full of stewed badger's lights, would dare to set foot. How would Mr Whitelaw 'recreate' something which never existed? The whole thing is a mystery, an example of demented Tory fantasizing quite as grotesque as anything ever dreamed up by Mr Benn's supporters.

DENIS THATCHER became one of the great characters in English comic fiction. He was always on top form during the Tory party conference, not least in 1982 at Brighton.

He explained how he planned to spend the conference period. 'I shall spend the first day here, then I have two days of board meetings in London, then back for the Boss's speech, then two more days in London, then I'm off with my friends to the Algarve. Golfers' paradise, old chap. Trouble is, nobody told me about this Falklands Victory Parade, so I shall have to miss a day.'

It does seem distinctly unfair that nobody told the Prime Minister's husband about the Parade, but then he does have quite a lot to put up with. For instance, he didn't like China one bit. Asked how it had struck him, he buried his chin in his chest, then raised it, lifted his eyebrows, and with the air of one imparting a great secret, said: 'Communist!' My informant, catching his drift, asked: 'Pretty awful then?' and Mr Thatcher agreed: 'Bloody! Of course, I've seen it before, Yugoslavia, East Germany, China, all the bloody same. Grey, drab conformity. I don't care where it is, socialism, communism, the lot, doesn't bloody work.'

He was, however, very grateful for the solicitude of his hosts. 'They housed us very well, little lake, potted plants,' but concluded, 'China—you can take it.'

He was, however, tremendously enthusiastic–like many of us–about Hong Kong. 'Marvellous place,' he said. As for Japan, it was remarkable for its splendid golf courses.

'D'you know what? All the holes have got *two* greens! I said to the chap I was playing with, 'What's the membership?'' and what d'you think it was? £175,000! And the green fees are £100 a day. So that's £5,000 a year just for a game on Sunday.'

One problem he found was that at the nineteenth hole, in spite of the phenomenal fees and in spite of the hot, muggy weather, there was no beer available, only tea. He had even survived the raw fish.

'We've got raw fish here too, you know, whelks, mussels, that kind of thing,' he added.

On a plane up to Scotland, on another occasion, the Thatchers were offered drinks by the stewardess. The Prime Minister asked for an orange juice and her helpmeet ordered a gin and tonic. 'Denis,' she said sternly, 'isn't it a bit early for a gin and tonic?'

Denis didn't hesitate. 'Darling,' he said firmly, 'it is *never* too early for a gin and tonic.'

THERE IS SOME splendid bitchiness in Mrs Thatcher's cabinet. Jim Prior was once asked his opinion about the Health Secretary Norman Fowler. 'There is a man who has been promoted above his station,' said Prior. 'And what is his station?' his friend inquired. With a curl of the lip Prior said: 'Coulsdon South.'

Long before the miners' strike, Arthur Scargill
became a figure of myth almost as evocative as
Denis Thatcher.

THE FUSS about Arthur Scargill reminds me that the myth of his popularity among miners has, sometimes, been exaggerated. For example, some years ago I found myself in the Fiesta Club, Sheffield, in the company of a most hospitable Labour MP. The Fiesta is a working men's club which manages to be both cavernous and intimate, as if the London Palladium were fitted out with little tables and lamps. Dinner cost £1, and on this occasion the star was the Manchester comedian Bernard Manning.

At the end of his act he leaned on the microphone and said, 'Arthur Scargill? Arthur Scargill? I'll tell you what I'd like to do with Arthur Scargill,' and he leered at us meaningfully. My host muttered: 'They won't like this, you know, Arthur Scargill is King around here.' Manning continued: 'I'd like to tek 'im out, buy 'im the hottest curry in Sheffield–and sew his arsehole up.' The audience collapsed with laughter and delight as we crept quietly from our table.

NEWS OF Tam Dalyell, Old Etonian and the only member of the Parliamentary Labour Party whose home is open to the public. There is a place in northern Scotland called Fyvie Castle, an historical relic which was about to be sold. A number of people were worried that it might fall into the wrong hands and so were organizing a campaign to save it for the nation. One of those most closely involved was a folk singer called Marc Ellington, who used to be with a group called Fairport Convention.

Anyhow, Tam decided to go up and see the place for himself. He was met at the station by Mr Ellington, who was driving a fine vintage Bentley. 'Oh dear,' said Tam, 'I don't want to ruin your carpet.' So before clambering into the back of the car he took off his shoes.

31

But when they arrived at the castle he forgot to put them back on again, and walked out of the car, across the mud, grass and gravel, in his stockinged feet. Some time later when he emerged from the castle he was wearing the same filth encrusted socks, carrying the pair of shoes before him.

THE SPLIT in the poor Labour Party is now so great that its MPs will lose no opportunity whatever to abuse each other, whenever and however they can. One day moderate left-wing Brixton MP John Tilley appeared on a local radio phone-in programme. At one point a caller rang in and identified himself as 'Arfur, from Westminster'. 'Arfur' said that he thought Mr Tilley's remarks a 'load of old rubbish' and inquired why he didn't shut up. He said this at some length. MPs appearing on the radio are, of course, accustomed to such attacks and Mr Tilley thought no more of it.

Until, that is, a couple of hours later, when he was back at the Commons to vote. He heard a voice behind him which sounded horribly familiar. He turned round and saw that it was indeed 'Arfur from Westminster'–Arthur Lewis, the (soon-to-be-ousted) MP for Newham North-west. Mr Tilley challenged him: had he been the mysterious abusive caller? 'Yeah, what if I was?' replied the silver-tongued Lewis. 'I was sitting in my office here and I thought what a load of rubbish you were spouting. So I phoned up to tell you.'

Leon Brittan, to everybody's surprise, became Home Secretary after the 1983 election. Like so many others, he owed his success to the patronage of his greatest fan, Willie Whitelaw.

WITH SEX-AND-POLITICS scandals, it doesn't so much matter what you do – the activity seems to be similar in all cases – but the way you set about it. Cecil Parkinson *looked* like a Lothario. He said risqué things to women he hardly knew,

Leon Brittan
in
MODERN TIMES

and generally behaved as if he wore brothel-creepers the way that Geoffrey Howe wears Hush Puppies.

Leon Brittan, by contrast, always looked like the bloke in the sixth form who never had a date. As a young man he used to go on holiday with older friends and their families. So, when he was adopted as the Tory candidate in Cleveland, nobody expected that he would take up with the wife of one of his new constituents. Indeed, he is now himself happily married to this lady. But behaviour which a hundred years ago would have, at best, ruined his political career and, at worst, caused him to be horsewhipped as far as Whitby, scarcely raised an eyebrow. The point being not that Brittan was any more moral than Parkinson, but that he didn't appear to be looking for it.

EVEN WHILE FRANCIS PYM was still a loyal member of the cabinet, Tory MPs were beginning to resent Mrs Thatcher's demands on them: 'She rewards slobbering and she punishes non-slobbering' a close colleague says. I learned why Geoffrey Rippon, surely one of nature's most ardent right-wingers, has never received government office under Her. During the leadership election in 1975 he spoke to a meeting of farmers in Hexham, his constituency. There were, I believe, six people present: five farmers and a young woman.

At one point Rippon was asked about the leadership. He said: 'I have no objection to a woman being leader of our party. But I have every objection to that woman.'

It was just his tough luck that the young lady in the audience was a *Guardian* reporter. His remark appeared prominently in that paper, and Rippon, once a cabinet minister, has spent the whole of the Thatcher years grumbling on the side-lines.

ANOTHER STORY from the further recesses of the Thatcher past. It comes from a neighbour of hers in Chelsea, and dates from over 25 years ago when the Thatcher twins were in their infancy. The neighbour says 'My wife often used to meet her taking the children for a walk. She always seemed so calm, so much in control. My wife felt terribly incompetent by comparison. While other mothers tend to scream at their children: 'Don't do that or I'll smack you!' she would say in that frightfully calm, measured way: "Now, Mark, you mustn't poke that stick in your sister's face, or she won't grow up to be a pretty little girl."

'On one occasion my wife was invited with our children round for tea at the Thatchers'. Because there were visitors, she had baked and iced a cake–in the shape of Windsor Castle.'

Less than a year after the Falklands War the Defence Secretary, John Nott, resigned, to be succeeded by Michael Heseltine.

MR HESELTINE made a resolute start to his tenure at the Ministry of Defence. He was explaining to a meeting of his ministerial colleagues a brilliant new plan to increase the sales of our armaments. A ship was to set off around the Mediterranean loaded to the gunwales with sample instruments of death–rockets, mortars, rifles and so forth–all of them made by British craftsmen. Eyes and hair alike gleaming, Heseltine explained that the vessel would call only at ports in countries of which our Government approved, such as Tunisia, Spain, Morocco, Greece, Turkey and Jordan. 'But, er, Michael, Jordan is completely landlocked,' said one of the ministers (my informant tells me it was Leon Brittan). Heseltine looked peeved at this petty cavilling.

'Well!' he said, I have only been in this job a week!'

IT WAS EARLY IN 1983 that the worrying signs of Mrs Thatcher's eccentricity began to appear. In the New Year she gave a number of television and radio interviews. One of those present was Peter Allen, who is the political correspondent of Independent Radio News. Mr Allen is not one for the hushed and reverential manner, and he successfully contrived to annoy her with a probing question about her Buy British campaign.

She promptly complained that he was using a Japanese microphone. Then, as is her wont, she decided to do the job properly and also demanded to know where his suit came from. He looked inside the jacket and said, 'It's rather embarrassing, Prime Minister. It says "Made in Romania".' Triumphantly, she cried: 'Come here, we shall tape that question again!' Mr Allen, correctly, refused. Prime Ministers are accountable to the public for their words and their deeds, not for the labels sewn into hacks' couture.

Faced with his refusal, she pulled off her shoe, like a female Nikita Krushchev, and waved it in the air. 'Look,' she cried, 'made in Norwich!' A cameraman came into the room and began to set up a tripod.

'Where did you get that tripod?' she demanded. The wretched man had to get down on his hands and knees before being able to mutter: 'Made in Bury St Edmunds, Prime Minister.' Finally she turned to Chris Moncrieff, the hard-working correspondent of the Press Association.

'Where did you get your suit?' she inquired.

'Burtons,' he replied.

'Goodness me,' she said, with that silver tongue so many of her ministers have come to love, 'I thought they had started making *snappy* suits.'

So it is a pleasant irony that Mr Moncrieff was one of the tiny handful of reporters who accompanied her to the Falklands. The Prime Minister prefers to have her hair done at least twice a week, and there is no hairdresser on either of the islands. She had to take a set of heated rollers in order to perform a DIY job on her own tresses.

36

'And I have to tell you that they are *Danish*,' she admitted, shame-facedly, to the delighted hacks.

THE VISIT TO THE FALKLANDS was accounted an enormous success and may have guaranteed her re-election.

You may have seen the TV pictures of her loosing off one of the cannon, which are mounted on the islands in order to deter Johnny Gaucho from making another cowardly attack on the plucky kelpers. To fire this particular gun, you have to sit on a metal seat, rather like those big lawn-mowers. She turned anxiously to the bombardier who was instructing her and asked 'Will this thing jerk me off?' He was able to reassure her.

At one point, the official party had to go inside a military tent.

'It's nice in a tent, isn't it?' Denis said.

One of the hacks told him. 'I don't know, I've never tried it.'

On an earlier trip Denis had journeyed down to the press end of the RAF plane in order to get a drink and have a chat about his favourite subject, golf. The RAF is the best airline in the world, not least because the stewardesses leave the bottles with passengers so they can help themselves.

Denis poured himself a refreshing gin. After a brief chat about birdies, eagles and the British Open, the company heard the dread footfall on the aircraft's gangway. She appeared.

'I thought there was going to be no gin on this trip,' she said.

'Oh no,' he replied gaily, 'it's not gin, only tonic!'

WE RECEIVED a continuing supply of 'Willieisms' from Viscount Whitelaw.

Mr Whitelaw does not specially like meeting members of the Conservative Party, and tends to go onto automatic pilot when he has to be nice to them. Certainly 'George' must

37

have been in control on a recent occasion when Willie was being introduced to a long line of party workers and worthies. As he shook each hand he said: 'Splendid, splendid, delighted to meet you, how are you?' At one point he said to an elderly woman: 'And how are *you*?' The woman replied: 'Not very well, actually, my husband died last week,'

'Splendid, splendid, keep up the good work!' he replied.

ENOCH POWELL has discovered an effective means of shutting up his fellow members of the Conservative Philosophy Group. This is a collection of pretentious Tories who meet in the hopes of constructing an intellectual scaffolding for Thatcherism—not an easy task, since the philosophy of Thatcherism amounts to what is in the Prime Minister's head at any one time and is no more a coherent system of thought than Nora Battyism would be.

Naturally most of the group's members like to spend their time scoring points off other members. They do this by asking cunning and allusive questions which, with any luck, their victim won't be able to answer. Powell has got around that one, however. Asked a weasly question, he began: 'As the Hebrew philospher said . . .' and gave the rest of the answer *in Hebrew*. There were no more questions.

I MET AN OLD COLLEAGUE of Tony Benn's from his youth, around 30 years ago, when he used to work for the BBC. He was a producer in Bush House, where he made programmes for the North American service. In those days talks and interviews were not recorded on magnetic tape but onto acetate discs, rather like instant gramophone records. As the broadcaster talked, the needle cut a groove in the disc, turning up a long thin coiled ribbon of acetate, known as 'swarf'. Swarf was highly inflammable.

On one occasion, the young Benn tapped out his pipe into a waste bin that was full of the stuff. The ensuing conflagration gutted the studio. From then on he was known at Bush House as 'Firebug Benn'.

The 1983 Bermondsey by-election was one of the dirtiest in recent memory.

IT IS A MYTH that the Liberals fought a clean campaign in Bermondsey. Naturally it wasn't remotely as bad as that conducted by John O'Grady, the 'Real Bermondsey Labour' candidate, who toured the streets singing a song which began: 'Tatchell is a poppet, as pretty as can be' and continued with a line about: 'He wears his trousers back to front . . .' However, some Liberals could be seen wearing badges which read: 'I haven't been kissed by Peter Tatchell.' It takes a lot of neck for Liberals to accuse other politicians of homosexuality.

As it happens, Tatchell's support for gay rights seems to have mattered a great deal less than a lot of his opponents hoped. There are, by now, quite a few homosexuals in parliament; they are, along with lawyers, one of the most over-represented groups at Westminster. (Though I suppose if you accept the absurd one-in-five figure which gays like to bandy about, this might not be the case.) Twenty years ago an MP who was caught with a guardsman in the bushes around St James's park would be an ex-MP before the case came up. Nowadays MPs can be plastered all over the court and social pages of the *News of the World*, or leave a public lavatory to be arrested by a whole division of flatfeet, and their general management committee calls a special meeting to award them a vote of confidence. What appears to have harmed Tatchell most was the fact that he was Australian, a new form of prejudice known, I suppose, as antipodeanism. A lot of Labour canvassers were startled and baffled when they heard people say, 'I'm not voting for that bloody Australian.'

TATCHELL'S OWN CAMPAIGNING methods were not always helpful. He affected a broad Cockney accent and used to go about shabbily dressed as if on his way to a sewage farm, or

Greenham Common. Then, with glottal stops burping up into his speech like a child who has just drunk a gallon of fizzy lemonade, he would say: 'My name's Peter Tatchell. I live on the Rockingham Estate, and I'm a bit of a rebel. Well, you've got to be a rebel if you're working-class and you live round here, haven't you?'

As one Labour voter muttered to a reporter shortly after Tatchell had left: 'If he can't get 'isself off the Rockingham Estate, what the hell can he do for us?' It's my experience that voters like their MP to be a bit of a nob, to give the impression that he can get things done, that he knows the right people. Anyone who went to live on the Rockingham Estate of his own accord must, by definition, be soft in the head.

All Tory home secretaries, especially wets like Mr Whitelaw, are under constant pressure from the Tory right. He countered with a barrage of deadly Willieisms.

WILLIE WHITELAW ended his altercations about the immigration rules, which involved him in several meetings with the right wing of the Conservative Party, about whom he has views roughly analogous to St Patrick's on snakes. I'm not sure about him, but I know his friends simply refer to them as the 'nasties'.

Just after the right wing had defeated him and the government, Willie held a meeting with the nasties. He outlined his new proposals in his usual florid Willie-speak and made it clear that he did not wish to win the vote simply on the abstention of the Labour Party. They had to vote for the new rules. 'So I hope you are content with what I have offered you!' he barked.

40

William Whitelaw
as Margaret Rutherford in ARABELLA

Ivor Stanbrook, the chief nasty, thought for a moment then, with a degree of wonderment, said: 'But you haven't offered us anything!

'Oh yes, I have,' said Willie. 'I am offering you a choice between minus one or minus two.' As is usually the case with Willieisms, those on the receiving end had to concede immediate defeat.

At another of these meetings, this one attended by a mixed bunch of different MPs, a furious argument began to rage. Willie cut in. 'Now then, stop, please stop, just a moment. Just wait . . . will you please excuse me?' Silence fell for a moment as Willie continued: 'I am about to lose my temper.'

The new left-wing labour boroughs in London spent much of their time questing for ideological purity—often managing to upset the very people they imagined they were supporting.

ANYONE WHO HAS worked in Belfast or Derry during the troubles will have noticed how some of the Republican 'freedom fighters' are as racist as anyone you might meet in the East End of London. They save their nastiest taunts for black soldiers: 'We'll melt yer down for rubber bullets,' is one of their milder slogans. So I suspect that some of the Irish in north London will have been particularly incensed by a slip of the tongue made by a local councillor who was explaining Brent's decision to discover the racial origin of anyone who applied for a job with them.

'We shall ask,' the left-wing councillor explained on Radio 4, 'whether they are black, Asian, Irish or white.'

FILIBUSTERING was raised to a new art form, unusually for our parliament. One record is held by a labour MP. Even his worst enemies, and there are lots of those, admire John Golding, the Labour MP for Newcastle-under-Lyme. Mr Golding is not an amateur politician, no wine-sniffing bibliophile who looks on the governance of Britain as a part-time hobby. He is, beneath his irreversibly shabby exterior (he feebly attempts to improve things with the occasional new suit and clean shirt, but they don't work; the minute he puts them on they look like Canadian army surplus tarpaulin), a tough and efficient operator.

He caused a lot of fuss by making a speech on Clause 3, Amendment 42 of the Telecommunications Bill. The speech was made to the members of Standing Committee H which has been considering the bill. It lasted for eleven and a quarter hours.

With a few short breaks for refreshment, Mr Golding's contribution to the debate went on from Tuesday afternoon until 5.20 on the following Wednesday morning. It was a new record for the British parliament.

The scale of Mr Golding's achievement becomes clear only when you realize the rules and restrictions under which he was operating. Unlike the United States Congress where filibustering Southern senators were once able to delay civil rights legislation by reading out their local phone directories, the Commons insists that every remark must be relevant, and that repetition is entirely out of order. MPs tend to get angry if you accuse them of filibustering, which, they say, is simply a crude and artless stratagem. Talking a bill out, the technical term for what they do in Britain, requires skill and verbal dexterity.

It is a little like the panel game *Just a Minute* except that challenges, instead of helping the other side, actually aid the speaker by spinning the proceedings out. At one in the morning, for instance, Tory MP John Lee tried to shut up Mr Golding with this intervention:

'I understand that repetition is not in order . . . but Mr Golding used the words "Miss Fookes" once at 12.36, once at 12.37, five times at 12.39, twice at 12.40 . . . and four times at 12.50. It seems to me, as a fair-minded person, that such a degree of repetition should render the honourable gentleman out of order. He clearly has nothing new to contribute.'

The chairman (Miss Fookes) replied: 'Accusations of tedious repetition usually relate to the substance of the speech, not to the honourable member addressing the chairman.'

An old hand like Golding wouldn't let a chance like that flash past. He kept the debate on whether he ought to address the chairman by name going for another five minutes or so.

In these circumstances you can't actually introduce your own personal irrelevancies, but you can cash in on other people's. At one point some members of the committee decided that the electric fan was making too much noise. The discussion on this continued for about ten minutes. Early in his speech, Mr Golding mentioned how he and his colleagues had broken for 'dinner'. Tory MP Richard Shepherd made the mistake of muttering to himself 'lunch'. Golding pounced. 'The way that southern gentlemen fall to the fly every time does not surprise me. As my honourable friends know, to us working-class northerners, dinner is dinner, whereas a meal at 1 o'clock is obviously lunch to southern gentlemen . . .'

One useful hint to speakers is to get hold of a secret document. This can then be quoted at pitiless length. Leavisite analysis of each paragraph means that you can spin out fifteen minutes' verbiage from every sentence. Mr Golding had obtained a private British Telecom briefing paper. He read out, as far as I can judge, every single word.

By 10.45 at night he was beginning to flag slightly. Then he spotted the Minister, Kenneth Baker, groping in his suit pockets.

Mr Golding: Is the minister clutching at straws?

Mr Baker: I am trying to find my cough sweets.

Mr Golding: I have never heard the like, Miss Fookes. . .

44

Mr Marlow: Get on with it.

Mr Golding: I accept for once the reprimand. It is a bit off-putting to be told by the minister that he is passing his time looking for his cough sweets. I wonder what *Erskine May* [the bible of parliamentary procedure] would say about sucking gobstoppers in a committee. I am sure that it would be considered out of order.

But Mr Golding's greatest skill is not in seizing these brief and fleeting opportunities to change the subject. It is his ability to talk for nearly twelve hours *on* the subject, which, on the remote chance that you might be interested, I can reveal was whether or not the new, privatized, phone service would charge customers different rates according to where they lived.

By midnight he was on to the higher cost of living for people who live on farms. At 1 am he was tackling the short-comings of a particular tariff reduction scheme. By 2 am he was vigorously assailing the suggestion that British Telecom should not have the maintenance contract for telephone equipment. Just before 3 am the committee took a break, but Mr Golding was steaming ahead on the subject of comparative national and international price structures. Half an hour later they were back, and Mr Golding was eloquent on the topic of rural areas: would they suffer because people living there made fewer phone calls? At 5 am he considered the special situation in Wales. A quarter of an hour later he rounded the speech off with some thoughts on other, similar, amendments, which had also been put forward. At 5.22 he sat down.

*From a newspaper's point of view, the sad fact
about the 1983 general election was that it
began as a foregone conclusion. This did not
make the campaigning either less vigorous or
less absurd. Highlights included:*

WALSALL MARKET, on a bustling weekday afternoon. The
place was full of sharp salesmen offering rubbishy goods at
impossible prices. 'Lissen, it's not gonna cost you a tenner,
it's not even gonna cost you a fiver. And here's what else I'm
prepared to throw in as a *gift.* . . .' And that was the politicians. The people selling cheap crockery and improbable
kitchen implements inspired more confidence.

Denis Healey was the star turn. As he moved about
people recognized him instantly. "Ere, it's him,' they said
to each other. 'He's on telly. Whatsis name?'

Mr Healey found a group of young men hanging about.
'Wotcher, boys' he said heartily. He always gives the impression that he learned his slang from a Berlitz course; somehow it's never quite right. It was disappointing to find that
one of the boys had a paid job, making burglar alarms. 'For
the nobs, I suppose' Mr Healey said wearily. Naturally
socialists like him don't have burglar alarms, even to protect
their Sussex mansions. Instead, strategically placed copies of
Labour's 'New Hope for Britain' persuade housebreakers to
abjure the life of crime.

The shadow Foreign Secretary was ruthless in his attempts
to salvage the election single-handed for Labour. He'd
agree about anything with anyone, even Michael Foot. A
stallholder said 'I'm sorry about the weather.' 'It's certainly
pissing down' he mused.

To a shopper, apropos of nothing, 'You know the great
message, don't you? "Be Alert. Britain Needs Lerts".'

'Go on, admit it, you think I'm Mike Yarwood,' he said to
some more youths. A timid schoolgirl was addressed: 'Do
you know who I am, with the eyebrows? Yes, you win the
prize!' He seem popular with the voters, perhaps because he

46

is never unwilling to make a fool of himself, whether on TV or in a market place. He'll do anything for a good picture. Asked to go behind a greengrocer's stall, he said 'All right' and started serving fruit. He found two five-year-old girls, neat and fragile in their blue school uniform. Placing his massive red face between theirs, he started chatting. The photographers wouldn't stop until he'd finished, and he didn't want to end until they had all the pictures they wanted, so the conversation went on and on, finally taking a surrealist turn. 'Can you read then? . . . can you count? Can you count backwards? . . . so you do ballet dancing, do you? Never do ballet with an elephant. Great big thumping things . . .'.

THE MOST HATED man in Britain drank his coffee with much satisfaction. 'If we win,' he remarked with his celebrated mirthless smile, 'we can thank the Dirty Tricks Department at Conservative Central Office. They've switched prescriptions. Foot's on the valium and Healey's got the benzedrine.' Outside the thunder rolled in from Essex, and the sky blazed with sheet lightning. It was a fitting setting for a walkabout by the Prince of Darkness. Norman Tebbit had come among his own.

Like most political demons, he is in reality an agreeable, fairly diffident sort of fellow. He is clearly very popular in Chingford. At times pensioners queued up to shake his hand. However, the rough edge of his tongue is always ready for instant action. One woman who complained about the price of vegetables was briskly told to grow her own. He justified cuts in education spending thus: 'We've taken the money away from the people who write about ancient Egyptian scripts and the pre-nuptial habits of the natives of the Upper Volta valley.'

Both the Labour and Tory parties need the image of Norman as a hate-filled thug. So must he, since he encourages it, perhaps because it masks his natural shyness. A Liberal worker handed him a huge envelope marked

'A Challenge to Norman Tebbit.' 'Put that in the bin, Renée,' he said to his agent.

This began a fierce battle of their loud hailers, as the Liberal candidate and the Tory campaign car tried to drown each other out. The cacophony must have been heard on Hackney Marshes. 'I challenge you a third time, Mr Norman Tebbit,' bellowed the Liberal. In these parts, voter feedback means a 120 decibel screech. Finally, in an effective display of unilateral disarmament, Mr Tebbit asked the Tories to stop.

His image would have been badly tarnished by an encounter with a housewife who wanted to know why the GLC could advertise for coloured workers, but she couldn't ask for a white cleaning lady. She got a detailed lecture on the need for positive discrimination. 'It's undoubtedly true that there is more unemployment among black people than among whites. . . . I think we must give them a fair crack of the whip.' The woman still looked doubtful. In Chingford, there were people who saw Norman Tebbit as a soggy Liberal.

It began to rain, so I sheltered in one of the many quaint old video shops which line Station Road. The first rack held the 'nasties': 'Zombie Creeping Flesh,' 'Microwave Massacre.' Outside, Norman was explaining that we lived in a hungry world and we must work to feed it. He was beginning to sound like Ted Heath. The next film was called 'Nightmares in a Damaged Brian'.

IN BRISTOL, Jonathan Sayeed was trying to beat the second most hated man in Britain, Tony Benn. Mr Sayeed was a smooth young man who described himself as a 'shipping and insurance consultant.' People had been saying that if there were a Tory landslide Parliament would be full of hatchet-faced right-wingers. But it wouldn't. Instead, it would be given over to young men like Mr Sayeed, middle-of-the-road Tories, articulate, expensively groomed, very pleased with themselves, better at making money than things.

48

Benn had decided on an in-depth campaign. 'I don't think there's any case for shouting a slogan from a defective loud speaker and then disappearing in a cloud of dust. In an election like this, the Labour candidate is a reassuring presence. People know that, whatever happens, we'll go on fighting for them.' One result was that the planned discussions of the issues often become ambles down memory lane. 'You meet people who are fat and old and bald, and they say: "Do you remember, you gave me a prize at school?" '

At a meeting that night, a man tried a trick question about private education and freedom of choice. Benn smoothly brushed him aside. 'If I kept a private fire engine so I didn't have to call the fire brigade, and expected the ratepapers to pay for it, you would call that an outrage.' The meeting sighed with pleasure.

Benn told them to trust their own experience. 'You don't need to have an economics degree to know when you've lost your job.' Like many successful politicians, Mrs Thatcher among them, he tells people that their instincts are okay; what they already feel is right.

(Jonathan Sayeed won.)

TWELVE MILES from Bristol, in Bath, two of Britain's most extreme moderates were slugging it out in a viscious, winner-takes-all battle. The Tory was Chris Patten, probably the best known and most articulate of all the wets outside government. The SDP candidate was Malcolm Dean, one of the scores of *Guardian* leader writers who were standing in the moderate cause across the country.

The SDP is perhaps the party of People Who Used To Be Quite Famous. A 'Stars For Dean' rally in the Pump Room included Margaret Drabble, Michael Young and Bamber Gascoigne.

Mr Patten was fighting a campaign of relentless energy. His canvassing trips were organized along the lines of an SAS raid. The cavalcade would screech to a halt, and immediately nine party workers, including his wife Lavender, fanned out to the doors and started banging on them all at once.

49

They were co-ordinated by a minder, a young man in a sports coat, who worked them like the drummer in a slave galley. A girl finished at one door. 'Okay, Dee Dee, *go*!' shouted the minder. The candidate hesitated at a privet hedge. 'Left, left, left, left! Mind that baby!' Precious micro-seconds were saved by jumping a wall instead of walking round it.

Mrs Patten found herself in a long conversation with an old man. 'Quick! Lavender needs *unlocking*!' shouted the minder. Patten ran up to every door at full speed. Had it opened suddenly, he would have disappeared and crashed into the greenhouse at the back. In a street of terrace houses, he saved entire minutes by holding two conversations at once.

These moderates were remorseless. One elderly gent said that he wouldn't be voting Tory. 'Well, whatever you do, you must use your vote. That's the important thing,' said Mr Patten. Encouraging his opponents to go to the polls. This man would stop at nothing.

MARVELLOUS to see you. So pleased to meet you. Very nice to meet you. Thank you very much!' Willie Whitelaw's electioneering technique might be described as 'hearts, minds and boomps-a-daisy'.

The campaign cavalcade, comprising Home Secretary, detectives, wife, daughter, grandsons, party workers and press, would roar into some Cumbrian fell village and scream to a halt. Peasants tried to flee, but it was too late. Willie was upon them, padding down their garden paths like a hungry grizzly. Sometimes they tried to ask a question, but this was neither the time nor the place.

It took about a minute to soften up the whole village. Then came the minds part of the operation. Willie picked up the public address system. This had the effect of making his voice quieter. Normally it can be heard in the next county.

The speech was always identical, and by polling day he must have delivered it between 200 and 300 times. 'The determined lead of Margaret Thatcher . . . dangerous world where we have to defend ourselves . . . strong, firm, united leadership . . . Willie Whitelaw, your Conservative candidate, asking you to re-elect me on June 9th. Willie Whitelaw, your Conservative candidate, re-elect me on June 9th, thank you very much!'

Finally, he took questions, and it must be said people got good value. In Hesket Newmarket, a man began 'Don't get me wrong, I'm not a racist. . . .'

He was of course, a racist. It's funny how people never begin: 'I am a racist, but I think we should let them all in . . .' The man got little comfort from Willie. His wife wanted a statutory minimum penalty for rape. Willie said this wasn't a good idea because there might be extenuating circumstances.

The wife, who had a hard face and narrow eyes, said: 'Mr Whitelaw, with rape there are no extenuating circumstances.' 'Oh, oh, oh, oh, oh, oh, oh! said Willie seven times. 'I am afraid I have to tell you that there are! Thank you very much!'

At the seaside village of Allonby, an amiable drunk wandered up. 'Why, you old bugger, you!' he said, 'Last election I asked you in for a pint and you said "No, sorry".'

'Well, the awful thing is that I'm going to say "No, sorry" again, because I'm in a hurry!' Nevertheless he disappeared into the pub, emerging a minute later. 'I escaped my drunk', he confided, 'by my well practised technique of *having a pee*. You go in, and when they offer you a drink, you say: "No, I must have a pee".'

We visited a fun-fair in the resort of Silloth, where Willie sometimes plays golf. He refused free goes on the coconut shy, the big wheel and entry to 'Count Dracula's Tomb,' probably because he saw enough of Norman Tebbit in London.

A woman was worried about the bomb, and he talked at length about the Russian threat. 'Ooh, but I'm not a Communist,' the woman protested. 'I vote SDP.' Ah, yes, well, thank you very much, delighted to meet you, very

51

pleased to see you, thank you so much, thank you very, very much.'

(Willie won; but went to the House of Lords in July 1983.)

NEARLY 300 MILES away from the Lakes is Bettyhill, a remote village in Caithness and Sutherland, which is the most northerly constituency on the British mainland. The local Labour Party secretary is Mr Bellsy Mackay. As well as being party secretary, Bellsy keeps the village shop, is the postmaster and the ambulance driver, and works as a crofter. The bank sets up in his front room twice a week. When he retires, he will halve Sutherland's unemployment total.

It's not easy canvassing in the Highlands. Candidates in the cities can walk to meet the voters. Here they may have to drive for several hours. It was a bad time of year for meetings, since many people spend the long luminescent evenings cutting their peat for next winter. Finally, and worst of all, Highland courtesy forbids being so rude as to tell anyone you won't vote for them. For this reason, all three main candidates were certain they were going to win.

The Labour candidate was an agreeably truculent Glaswegian called Danny Carrigan, and Bellsy took us to meet some supporters. One of them had a local newspaper with the headline: 'Macduff Death: Man Detained,' a tribute to the tenacity of the police here.

It was all rather confusing for the voters, since in 1979 they voted for the Labour candidate, Robert MacLennan. He was one of the first converts to the SDP, and was now standing for that party.

All the candidates agreed to speak at a public meeting organized by the Church of Scotland and held in the Assembly Rooms, Wick. The subject was 'Moral Issues Raised By The Election.' The audience were a tough lot. Alcohol came early on the agenda. On the whole, the panel were against it.

52

'Alcohol is a substance many people enjoy at celebrations, weddings and so forth,' said Mr MacLennan piously, as if that was the only time he ever witnessed drink being taken. Alastair Scouller, the Tory, added: 'All of us have known people who have taken alcohol to excess . . .' as one might say: 'All of us have met opium fiends.' A man in the audience thought the police ought to breathalyze pedestrians as well.

These people think the permissive society means buying soap powder on a Sunday. One man had discovered that some people at the Dounreay nuclear power station actually work on Sundays.

'It is unprincipled that young men should be taking a holiday on Saturday and going to work on God's Day!' Mr Carrigan looked queasy. Mr MacLennan chipped in: 'For a Christian, the mandate is clear. Remember the Sabbath Day and keep it holy.' Mr Carrigan looked as if he would like to throw up.

The last subject was pornographic cable television. We held our breath waiting to see whether the candidates would be for it or against it. They were, it turns out, opposed to it, except for Mr Carrigan who was clearly near the end of his tether. 'I don't see why we should be worrying about video porn,' he growled. 'We haven't even got Channel 4 in Wick yet.'

(Mr MacLennan won.)

MANY OF HIS BEST FRIENDS are still baffled by Francis Pym's behaviour. Why did he decide that he would accept no job other than Foreign Secretary? Having taken the decision, why did he make it public? And why on earth did he make that remark about not wanting a landslide? Nearly all his colleagues agreed heartily with what he said but were appalled by the fact that he said it. It was like saying to all the Tory candidates in difficult seats: 'Not only do we not expect you to win, we would rather you didn't.'

One of his friends did offer an explanation. He blamed the

atmosphere at the BBC's 'Question Time' programme, where Pym's mistake was first made: 'It's surprisingly intimate there. You have a few drinks with Robin Day and all the other people on the panel, the audience are very close, so that you really feel you are talking to them. Somehow you forget that the cameras are there. With Robin pressing you to be indiscreet the whole time it's very hard not to be unless you keep a tight hold on yourself.'

JIM CALLAGHAN in 1979 went on his famous 'Avoid the People' election tour of Britain. It was a brilliant success, and Labour won no fewer than 268 parliamentary seats. I hoped to find the same dazzling technique in his own Cardiff seat in 1983, and I could not have been luckier. Like watching Karajan conduct or Jack Nicklaus golfing, here was one of the greatest of the old pros.

There was neither hide nor hair of him on the St Mellons estate, where he was supposed to be. His agent, Jack, now Lord, Brooks, said to look out for a white minibus with red stickers. Finally I saw the vehicle, which was stopping every few minutes for the driver to harangue the public. It turned out he was selling ice cream and hadn't seen Mr Callaghan.

A small boy had a 'Jim's The One' badge of his jumper. 'He went off somewhere. It was a long time ago,' he said. I plunged back into the estate. Not only was there no sign of him; I couldn't find anyone else who'd met him. It's heartwarming to watch such art.

'He's gone back home,' Brooks told me when I called on him at lunchtime. 'He won't be out again till much later.' It's typical of a foxy old campaigner like Jim to wait till dark. That way he runs even less risk of the voters spotting him.

'Has he gone for a nap?' I enquired. 'I expect so,' said Brooks. I asked about his plans for the following day. 'Ah yes, here's the diary for tomorrow,' Brooks said, showing it to me. It was completely blank.

54

SO MANY HUMILIATIONS were heaped on poor Michael Foot through the election campaign that, paradoxically, the man's essential dignity shone through more brightly than ever. In Nottingham he was interviewed by a nervous local radio chap, who said: 'We are very pleased to see Michael Foot here, especially because I was the reporter at his terrible car crash in 1963, and the surgeon said to me, "Nothing human could have come out of this crash".' The journalists who followed his tours around the country called the party the 'Worzelcade'. David Steel's Liberal battle bus was, of course, known as the 'Blunder Bus'.

A magazine called the *Finchley Leader* was devoted entirely to the greater glory of Margaret Thatcher. Or at least to convincing the voters of Finchley that while she may be Prime Minister, her real over-riding interest was in that north London borough. For example, it listed among her qualities: 'leadership, courage, foresight, compassion, concern and dedication to Finchley ...' Photographs showed her in China, attending the Council of Europe and 'querying the price of a grapefruit with a street trader in North Finchley'. Among the twenty-three pictures of Margaret Thatcher which figured in the four-page paper, my favourite showed her with a demented smile talking to an elderly Asian woman at an old folk's home. The lunatic caption read: 'Mrs T. at the Grange. A regular annual visit to the Old People's Christmas Party at the Grange estate in December 1982. One senior citizen asked: "How do you manage to get here every year?" Mrs Thatcher replied: "I tell the world leaders they cannot meet me this weekend unless they come to the Grange Estate." And she meant it!' If the voters of Finchley believed that, they'd believe Denis Thatcher is a teetotaller.

A FEW INSIGHTS into why the Labour Party did so appallingly badly in the last election: friends of mine live in Dulwich, a marginal seat, and decided to offer their help to Kate Hoey, the Labour candidate. So they called at the committee rooms, where they were met by a youth with shoulder-length hair, wearing bright orange ankle-to-neck overalls, so, they said, he looked a bit like Ronald McDonald in the hamburger ads. 'No, no, we don't need any help,' he told them, 'it's all middle-class where you live.' But, they protested, they hadn't seen a single canvasser. 'That's right, we're concentrating our efforts,' said the youth, showing them the door. Not typical of Dulwich, I gather, but symptomatic of a wider malaise.

Louis Heren, former deputy editor of *The Times*, and a lifelong Labour supporter, offered his help to the party headquarters in Walworth Road. He hoped they might have a job for him helping with the press. Naturally he offered his services free. Naturally, being the Labour Party, they refused.

Jim Callaghan was canvassing in Cardiff, a marginal seat. A small boy answered the door. 'Is your mother in?' asked the former Prime Minister. 'No,' said the erp.
'Do you know when she will be back?'
'No.'
'Do you know who I am?'
'No.'
'Dear, dear, dear me,' said Jim, as he wandered on his way. 'I wonder what on earth they teach the kids in school these days.'

ONE OF LABOUR'S election post-mortems was provided by Shadow Cabinet member Gwynneth Dunwoody. Some of her Labour Party colleagues were more than a shade startled to read her analysis of what went wrong–not least because Mrs Dunwoody, as chairman of the press and publicity committee, was directly responsible for much of it. And what a disaster it was. An issue of the *Journalist* contains a most revealing article by a Scottish reporter called Jim Innes, who worked for the party's press office during the campaign.

Mr Innes's revelations are often hilarious, though the smile must quickly die on the lips of anyone who is not a supporter of Mrs Thatcher. For example, there was almost no central planning of leaders' tours. If Innes wanted, say, Denis Healey to appear on a radio programme, he had to fight national, regional and constituency associations for his time. 'This means that for the next few weeks I work for the radio stations. The Tories manipulate *them*, and they manipulate me. The Labour Party just pays my wages.'

The Tories launched their manifesto on 18 May. Naturally the press wanted to know where to go for reactions from top Labour politicians. 'We tell them that they can go to Wales for Foot, or the North for Healey, or the Midlands for Hattersley . . . Thatcher takes the headlines for the third day in a row'

Michael Foot's tours took him to the most improbable places, often where Labour had not the faintest chance of winning. Innes says that the motto must have been 'Never mind the media, the mileage is the message.' He goes on: 'Foot's tours have a strange kind of Militant tendency. He's always bumping into the candidates with Bold Socialist policies. Andy Bevan, the full-time supremo of the Militant-controlled Young Socialists, is working in the National Agent's office. But there can't possibly be any connection.'

What with assistants and researchers, somewhere between thirty and forty people attended every meeting of the party's campaign committee held daily during the election. There were not enough chairs. 'One chap was in there for the first two days and nobody recognized him. On the third day someone asked who he was and he told them he was Foot's Special Branch detective. Given the make-up of the committee he was probably quite right to go in.' And they still have inquests into why they lost.'

ONE POLITICAL CURIOSITY is the way that MPs' best friends often come from the opposite party. There is a reason for this, neatly illustrated by the apocryphal story about the young Tory MP coming to the House for the first time. As he sits down he looks across the chamber and says to the old stager at his side: 'It's good to get a sight of the enemy.' His colleague says: 'No, my boy, you've got it wrong. That is the Opposition. The enemy is on this side.'

All the main parties are seething masses of rivalry, tension, hatred and contempt. Often it is only with someone from a different party that an MP can feel assured and relaxed.

Take the case of Walter Harrison, the Labour party's famously devious Deputy Chief Whip. He used to spend many a pleasant evening drinking and plotting with his old friend John Stradling Thomas who used to be the Deputy Chief Whip of the Conservative Party. He has since been promoted, in rank if not in influence, to number two at the Welsh Office.

A convivial raconteur, Mr Stradling Thomas used to be (a) a vet and (b), so he claims, a member of the Communist Party. When the citizens of Monmouth asked him to stand for parliament he had to inquire which party they had in mind. Though he is now a loyal Thatcherite, he is the only man in the House who can recite an entire Nye Bevan speech, including all the right gestures and little squeaky top notes.

Now he is gone from Mr Harrison's life, and it is a glummer Whip who stalks around the Commons these days. He does, however, have his reputation for chicanery to console him. He has probably pulled more fast ones than any other MP in our constitutional history.

Once he was playing at home with his young grandson. According to Walter, the boy got up and stalked off. His kindly grandfather asked him why. 'Because you've cheated at Ludo, you took a card off the bottom of the pack in Snap and you tried twice to change the rules in Happy Families.'

AS HER TERM OF OFFICE progressed, the Prime Minister's strange use of language was noted. Some thought her remarks were deliberate. Personally, I doubt if she would recognize a double-entendre if it walked up and handed her a Red Box. There was, for instance, the time that her campaign coach got stuck in the mud during the 1979 election. All the passengers leapt out to push it free.

Shrill cries of encouragement piped from the bus: 'Keep going, keep going, let's not stop until we get onto the hard stuff!'

On one occasion she was visiting an electrical repair shop in Fulham. Surrounded by large and loutish youths, some of whom have doubtless let slip the odd vulgarism after their second sarsaparilla, she spotted a Stanley screwdriver. 'What a peculiar tool!' I've never seen one as large as that!' she exclaimed, then looked puzzled when all around her collapsed with laughter.

Another example comes from the World Service of the BBC to which she paid a visit. This was shortly after it had been announced that the World Service would not be broadcast to Britain any more, and that the transmitters would beam the signal only in an abroadwards direction.

Mrs Thatcher marched briskly into the studios, and demanded: 'Why don't I get it at home any more?'

All MPs get letters, a thick pile several times a day.

DAVID STEEL keeps a special file of the strangest letters, some of which are funny, some bizarre, and some so weird that the smile dies upon the lips as you read. Here's a letter on child's patterned notepaper, though the writing is of an uneducated adult: 'Dear Mr Steel, I am writing to protest about the fact that I am pregnant–don't remember what happened to me. Dr is lousy. Can you please help me?' What depths of despair made that woman write to a politician, a figure on a television screen? Steel wrote back suggesting a call to the British Pregnancy Advisory Service, and short of sending a cheque for £1,000, there was nothing else that he could do.

The writing and the format of a letter are no guide to the extent of its loopiness. Here's one written in old fashioned curlicued handwriting signed 'British Citizen' and addressed to 'Dear David and all the Alliance'. It is an outpouring of hatred against the Conservative party ('Right-wing Tories are the scum of the earth. Thatcher, Tebbit, Howe etc they are worse than Hitler') though the writer's main objection seems to be that they are not keen enough on pornography. 'One thing which really makes me livid is that Thatcher grovels to sexually frustrated Whitehouse. Anything to do with sexual freedom and pornography (legal other countries) then Thatcher can't act fast enough to crush these, when porn is legal in other countries and Britain should have the same sexual freedom as Germany, Denmark, Sweden . . .'

The writer's real worry seems to be that he (or she; it isn't clear) has not been getting enough. 'Time and time again Tory MPs are mixed up in sex scandals. No laws against sex will worry them. Even if all sex were banned today Tory MPs would still wallow in porn & sex. Take the way poor Jeremy Thorpe was crucified. When anyone with brains knows House of Commons is riddled with homosexuals. I will name two now in Tory anti-sex Thatcher cabinet. (The writer then mentions two distinguished Conservatives, both of them happily married.)

I suspect that the pleasure is two-layered: the politician is presumed to rely on the votes of the public, and is therefore thought to be under a moral obligation to read anything the

David Steel
in
SORRY!

public sends, even if it arrives in the form of 28 pages filled with unreadable scrawl. But he is also believed to have power, and so your nostrums and your complaints might be acted upon. If they are not, then you have the delicious pleasure of righteous indignation. This too is a recurring theme of an MP's correspondence: fury that he has not awarded the merited weight to a letter.

Here's a man who got a perfectly courteous reply to a letter he had sent. He was quite correctly recommended to try his own MP. The letter, he writes in reply, 'is the rudest and most arrogant letter I have ever read. I have voted Liberal for the last time.' Here is a women who lives in an extremely expensive London street. She had written asking why the Liberals and the SDP did not join and form one party. Someone on Steel's staff had given a brief but informative resumé of the reasons for this.

'What an *absolutely typical* politician's *non-reply* to my letter,' she replied. 'You have told me nothing I didn't know already and your reply is exactly the sort of thing that makes the public despise and despair of politicians ... *If* you don't *know* the answer to my queries why not make a great effort to be *honest* and say so?' What people resent, I think, is not an inadequate response but the absence of a sudden conversion. The only acceptable reply would begin: 'Dear Madam, when I read your letter the scales fell from my eyes. You are, I now see, entirely correct ...'

Now this letter looks as if it should have been signed by Yosser Hughes. After several pages of abuse ('Your party is associated with failure and has offered the country the most pathetic policies ...') it ends: 'I could use a job if you have one spare.' What did the writer, a businessman from Cheshire, expect would happen? That Steel, pacing his tiny office, would cry: 'This man is right! We are failures! Our policies *are* pathetic! Thank God he's willing to work for us. Get him on the phone, offer him anything ...'

A squadron-leader with seventeen letters after his name (and 'Retd.') sends four pages of libel and slander from a village in Kent. 'Dear Mr Steel, it has been suggested to me that the majority of Liberals are either (a) PUFTAS (b) PERVERTS (c) LIBERTINES or (d) BORN GAMBLERS.' The missive continues with a dozen or so paragraphs of personal abuse against Steel himself, ending 'I would appreciate a personal reply, for the Family Album'.

Some letters begin 'Dear Mr Steel,' others kick off with a matey 'Dear David' and some try to wheedle favour, as in 'Dear Your Excellency.' The saddest of all starts: 'Dear Mr, I am enclosing herewith photo copies of my sworn affidavit and other documentary evidences concerning the con- spirators against my life together with their backers from the big officials of the Tory government . . .'

Journalists get letters like this too, often in vividly deco- rated envelopes which are designed to attract attention but succeed only in warning of a nutcase. But we get fewer, and the passions evoked seem, somehow, damper and more dis- couraged. I think if every day someone handed me so many small parcels of rage and despair I would be quite fright- ened, worried about what the end result might be. Or perhaps, like most MPs, I would despatch them all with a curt reply and hope they would vanish swiftly and forever from my life.

A TRIBUTE NOW to the wisdom and foresight of Roy Hat- tersley, who is one of the joint chairmen of an organization called 'Solidarity'. This exists to unite Labour right-wingers (or moderates, as they prefer to be known) and to conduct the counter-revolution against the New Left. The other joint chairman is Peter Shore.

On one occasion neither Hattersley nor Shore was able to attend the weekly Solidarity meeting at the House of Commons, owing to their pressing engagements elsewhere. To their considerable anger another of their colleagues, cigar smoking, football refereeing, camel-hair coated Dennis Howell, decided to record in the minutes his criticism of their absence.

63

Next week, the two victims waited for Howell to appear. He did not. Then they learned that he was at Wembley, sitting high in the grandstand, watching England's last international football match of the season.

Mr Hattersley promptly phoned the Royal Box and demanded to speak to Mr Howell. Mr Howell was dragged away from his comfortable seat, his friends and his panatellas. As he picked up the phone to answer, the line unaccountably went dead. Mr Hattersley waited a few minutes more (to make sure that Mr Howell was back and comfy in his seat) and repeated the exercise. Once more, to the bafflement of all present, the line went dead.

He rang a third time, having left, it goes without saying, ample time for Mr Howell to re-ensconce himself. This time he did not demand the former Minister for Sport. Instead he left an urgent message for him to ring the Houses of Parliament.

By this time Mr Howell was getting agitated. He immediately phoned back to the MPs' message service. Was he needed to take over the leadership of the Labour Party? Did Mrs Thatcher want him to join her in a Government of National Unity? Evidently not. The helpful person on the switchboard dug out the message: 'Mr Hattersley and Mr Shore are *very sorry* that you have not been able to attend the Solidarity meeting.'

THE PRIME MINISTER'S CONSORT continued to emerge as one of the great characters in English comic fiction. Mr Thatcher took a golfing holiday in Spain with his friend Bill Deedes. On the course they noticed a familiar figure who turned out to be the world-famous professional golfer Severiano Ballesteros. They challenged him to a game and were delighted when he won by only a small margin. Unfortunately one small fact took the gilt off their gingerbread: Ballesteros agreed to stand on one leg every time he hit the ball.

I AM SOMETIMES ASKED: can an MP be a wally? Naturally the answer is yes, though the numbers involved depend on your exact definition of the term, and slang is notoriously vague. I take a wally to be rather more than a fool. He is generally someone whose ambition to be admired and socially accepted outstrips his taste and judgment. In the non-political world a wally is a chap who wears lots of aftershave, has his family saloon car fitted with mag wheels and a 'spoiler' to reduce its drag coefficient, boasts about how many pints of lager he swilled down last night, wears chunky gold rings and rally jackets marked 'Team Marlboro' on the back, and says 'this is it' when he means 'yes'. Obviously there is some overlap between the ordinary workaday wally (who has no interest in politics) and the Westminster wally. For example, some MPs have absurdly overpowered sports cars to drive around city constituencies in which not a single street is outside the 30 mph limit. Others, though raised in middle-class suburbs, affect cockney slang ('ruby' for curry; 'tom' for jewellery) under the mistaken impression that they appear streetwise.

But, of course, there are several ways in which an MP can be uniquely wally, opportunities which do not exist for the rest of us. For instance, a wally MP has an opinion about every subject there is, and never misses a chance to express it. When you hear the news headlines: 'MPs lash out at the killer beer-mats,' or 'Labour MPs say Prince Charles should join the striking miners . . .' then you know that a wally has been sounding off.

Give him any topic you wish and the wally MP will bat it back as quickly as a 'Mastermind' contestant. 'Did the police riot in Belfast last Sunday?'; 'Is Boy George setting a bad example to Britain's youth?'– the wally is on to the Press Association in a blur of dialling digits. He knows their reporters' home phone numbers by heart. Now and again the wally manages to fool some radio programme into interviewing him and begins to see himself as an expert on the subject: 'Speaking as chairman of the all-party group on beer-mat safety. . . .' Oblivious to the sniggers of his colleagues and the journalists' nickname 'Dial-a-Quote,' he thinks of himself as a distinguished savant, a well-loved guardian of the nation's welfare.

As with all drugs, the craving for publicity begins to take its terrible human toll. After a few years, the wally has lost so much self-respect that he allows reporters to make up quotes and attach his name to them. He even lets them invent parliamentary questions which he then takes along to the Table Office for his fix.

A wally MP who talks about his constituents as if the psephological accident which made him their representative also blessed them with unparalleled powers of percipience. 'I can tell the minister this: the people of West Barsetshire at least will not be deceived ...'; 'Folk who live in Loamshire have an old-fashioned habit—we call a spade a spade ...' When his constituents come to the House the wally fusses over them like a hen, buys them drinks and makes a great show of regarding their predictable opinions as his personal hot-line to What The Nation Thinks. Most unkindly of all, he introduces them to his colleagues and to passing journalists (the wally puts great store by knowing the more famous hacks: 'As I said to Robin Day last week, "Robin," I said ...'). One of the most chilling sentences you can hear on the terrace or in the tea room is 'I'd like you to meet my constituency chairman'. The correct response to this grisly invitation is to praise the wally fulsomely, ending with an enigmatic line such as: '... and how well he coped with the drink problem,' or 'that silly business with the police'.

Wallies go on parliamentary free trips to places like the Seychelles and San Francisco, then bore on about them back home in order to imply they were doing a useful job of work. They know lots of foreign wally politicians, about whom they also boast: 'Jim Haddockhammer is a great friend of mine, and he's going to be the Democrats' presidential candidate in '92 ...' or 'Hans Saftsack was telling me in the Bundestag last week that his people won't stop Poland joining the EEC ...' The further he goes abroad, the less the

66

wally knows of home, and the more his prejudices are confirmed. For wally MPs, travel narrows the mind.

Wally MPs leer at their secretaries and try to imply that they are sleeping with them, though the secretaries despise the wallies and resent the fact that they pay them less than the full allowance so they can drink the rest. MPs are permitted to jump the Commons taxi queue, though only wallies do. They buy all their Christmas presents at the souvenir stand, believing that their relatives and constituents will be thrilled by a packet of House of Commons after-dinner mints. When they make a speech, they order a hundred extra copies of Hansard to send to their friends.

Labour wallies affect to be working-class even when they aren't. They wear open-neck shirts (sometimes even T-shirts) or polyester ties of a colour not found in nature. They drink hearty pints of beer and refer to all male persons as 'lads'. They talk about the Labour Movement as if it was an entity which actually existed, like the Football League. They boast about their friendship with such unloved people as Arthur Scargill and Gerry Adams.

Tory wallies say things like: 'It is a disgrace to attack the Royal Family, who cannot answer back.' They drop names such as Lord Cockfield and John Selwyn Gummer, and imagine that their listeners will be impressed. They belong to Annabel's and try, unsuccessfully, to inveigle female lobby correspondents there after the House has risen. But the greatest proof of their wally status, the absolute clincher, is that they praise Mrs Thatcher *in private*.

NIGEL LAWSON was promoted to glory shortly after the election. Tory backbenchers keep telling their friends what a pompous ass the Chancellor of the Exchequer is. I can't think why. I have always found him most stimulating and engaging. It could be, of course, that his colleagues are misled by what one might call, for want of a better term, Mr Lawson's manner.

He was selected by an important Fleet Street newspaper

as a Coming Man, along with several other leading Tories. The paper had arranged for a famous photographer to snap them on the Commons terrace. All of them appeared on time, and none of them gave any trouble except for Nigel.

'I wish to see the prints before they are published in your newspaper,' he announced.

'Do you know', said the famous photographer, 'that in my whole professional career only one other person has made that request?'

'And who might that have been?' asked Niglet.

'Zsa Zsa Gabor,' said the photographer, smiling sweetly.

GEORGE BROCK, co-author of the biography *Thatcher* draws to my attention another Thatcherism, this time one which illustrates her extraordinary sense of humour, or rather her lack of one. It came during the preparation of a party conference speech. This was to be delivered the week after Peter Jay had unwisely revealed that his father-in-law Jim Callaghan saw himself as Moses, leading the British people out of the wilderness. Chris Patten and Ronnie Millar, her speech-writers, suggested the line: 'So my message to Moses is, keep taking the tablets.' Not great, but not bad for a political speech.

The then Leader of the Opposition thought the audience wouldn't laugh. The two speech-writers assured her they would. The line went in and came out of the speech several times. I quote the book: 'In the middle of the night she returned to the subject and announced that she had thought of a better line: "So my message to Moses is: keep taking the pill!" In stunned silence the team realized that she had never understood the joke.'

THE PARLIAMENT was punctuated by disputes over the House of Lords. Mrs Thatcher wanted more pliant peers, and the Labour Party just wanted more peers. Even if

Nigel Lawson
in
THE GODFATHER

Labour got all the lords it wanted, the Conservatives would still have twice as many as Labour: four hundred, compared with not quite two hundred.

What Mrs Thatcher dislikes, of course, is the fact that the Tory peers are no longer certain to vote for the Tories. Sometimes they rebel, and vote against the party whips, on subjects such as school bus fares and local government.

It must all be very inconvenient for the government, but then that is the entire point of the House of Lords. It is put there to disagree with governments. If it always did what it was told, it might as well pack up and write its memoirs. Mrs Thatcher not only wants a two-to-one majority but she also wants a two-to-one acquiescent majority. This strikes me as greedy.

It is, I fear, part of her growing conviction that she is actually the Queen, and that the woman in Buckingham Palace is a pretender, an irrelevance like ex-King Zog of Albania. I offer two small indications of the way people perceive this.

During the election, voters showed an alarming tendency to refer to her as 'Ma'am'. This form of address is, of course, only used for the Queen. If you meet Mrs Thatcher, you should call her 'Prime Minister', though 'Mrs Thatcher' *tout court* will serve perfectly well.

Secondly, there is the report in the *Daily Express* of her meeting (described as a 'wigging') with Piet Dankert, president of the European Parliament. 'Speaking,' the report says, 'after the audience . . .' The *audience*? Perhaps she thinks she is the Pope, as well.

POLITICAL CLICHÉS change very fast, largely because the people who use them find them picked up by their opponents and flung back. A good example of this is the word 'compassion'. It was used by Labour politicians to congratulate themselves for using tax-payers' money to alleviate hardship. Now it is used mainly as a term of contempt by Tory right-wingers.

Now for a few other words whose meaning changes every five or ten years. Sometimes meanings overlap and you have to know who is speaking to understand his exact implication. Sometimes apparent synonyms have opposite meanings. Thus, 'freedom' is a right-wing term which means bashing the unions. 'Civil liberties' is a left-wing phrase used almost exclusively against policemen. I have put in brackets afte each word the group or groups which most commonly use it.

'Communist' (Con.): member of CND, any one who supports unilateral nuclear disarmament. Sometimes, though not often, it is acknowledged that such a person may not actually be yearning for the day when the Red Army marches through Bromley. In this case the correct phrase is 'Soviet dupe'.

'Cynical' (all parties): used of any policy or statement likely to be successful with the voters. Thus: 'The government's proposal to give a leather bag of golden sovereigns to every family in the land is a cynical ruse to manipulate the electorate. It is doomed to failure.' (That is, it is certain to succeed.)

'Defence' (Con.): exact opposite of 'peace' (q.v.).

'Democratic' (all parties, though mainly Lab.): system of voting which achieves the result which the speaker desires. For example, 'In a truly democratic union such as ours, the decision on who to support for the Labour leadership must be taken by the general secretary'. In the present day Labour Party 'democracy' generally means 'rule by a small number of dedicated activists'. This is sometimes described by the dedicated activists as 'the democracy of the committed'.

The opposite of this is 'armchair democracy', used by Moss Evans to describe a postal ballot. The implication that votes cast in a sedentary position are worthless enables Mr Evans to restrict the franchise to himself and his friends.

The phrase 'so-called democracy' means, naturally, a voting system which brings about the result the speaker does

71

not desire. Thus our present electoral system is described as 'so-called democracy' by the Liberals and the SDP, and by the far left.

'Difference of emphasis' (Con.): complete and total disagreement. If the Prime Minister says that the sun rises in the east and Mr Pym says it rises in the west, this is a 'difference of emphasis'. While I do not entirely agree that we should string up one striker in ten every week until they stop, I can assure you that this is nothing more than a difference of emphasis between the minister and myself.'

'Fascist' (Lab.): anyone to the right of Roy Hattersley. Sometimes used as synonym of 'Thatcherism' (q.v.). No relation to the Italian and German political systems of the thirties, which implied total subservience to the State by all sections of society. For example, whereas Mussolini made the trains run on time, Thatcher would happily see them disappear altogether.

'Iniquitous' (all parties): possibly on balance mistaken. 'The iniquitous decision to add 0.001 per cent to the national insurance surcharge will enrage the people of this country . . .'

'Labour movement' (Lab.): tiny groups of activists who claim to speak for all working men and women (q.v). 'Let the message go out from this great Labour movement of ours . . .' means 'from the half-dozen middle-class Trots who make up Bloggsbury Ward Labour Party'.

'Mandate' (all parties): whatever you can persuade yourself the electorate have voted for. Thus Mrs Thatcher's landslide gave her a mandate to install cruise missiles and buy Trident. But the fact that 54 per cent voted for parties which oppose both, gives them the opposite mandate.

'Peace movement' (CND, Lab., etc): those who believe that peace can best be secured by unilateral nuclear disarmament. The use of the word implies that those who do not agree are the 'war movement'. A typical variation occurs in names such as 'Journalists Against Nuclear Extermination' whose members presumably believe that those who do not support their strategy are heartily in favour of nuclear extermination. 'Peace' is the exact antonym of 'defence' (q.v.).

'Positive' (all parties): favourable, usually created by public relations. 'It is important that we give a positive impression of British intentions to the countries of Latin America . . .' means 'It is vital that we con them rotten about what we are up to.'

'Sectarian' (Lab.): refers to those in the same party who disagree with the speaker but refuse to admit that they are wrong.

'Socialist' (Lab.): set of beliefs adhered to by the speaker. Carries the implication that what other people believe isn't socialist.

'Socialist' (Con.): anyone left of Francis Pym.

'Thatcherism' (all parties): dogmatic, ideological belief in the virtues of the market economy. The Prime Minister is a fairly lukewarm example of a Thatcherite. She is surrounded by people who are 'plus Thatcheriste que la Thatcher'. The term, when applied to the individual Margaret Hilda Thatcher, is no more meaningful than 'Esther Rantzenism'.

'Tendency' (Lab.): see 'sectarianism'. Splinter group on the left claiming profound philosophical differences with other splinter groups; in fact created by personality clash between separate monstrous egos.

'Treasonous' (Con.): used of anyone who disagrees with Mrs Thatcher.

'Working man'; 'working classes' (all parties): used of the speaker and those who agree with him, e.g. 'as a working man myself' means 'as an extremely rich public relations consultant for a firm manufacturing poisonous chemicals'. In the Labour Party, generally used by polytechnic lecturers, journalists, trade union research assistants and lawyers to refer to themselves.

'Youth' (Lab.): generic term, both singular and plural like 'sheep', which means 'all persons under the age of thirty-five who might be thought to have done worse under a Tory Government'. The Tory term is 'young people' and has exactly the opposite meaning.

*An old chum is Eric Heffer, a thoughtful and
kindly man, burdened with an ego as big as all
outdoors:*

WE ALL GREATLY enjoyed the tone of rancid acrimony
which coloured the struggle for the Labour leadership. It
touched on everything. For instance, I gather that after the
news of Neil Kinnock's car crash came through, Eric Heffer
was seen wandering ruefully around Westminister pointing
out in hurt fashion that when *he* had a car crash, the press
hardly wrote a thing about it. 'And I didn't need a taxi to get
home,' he added proudly. 'I took the train.'

MR KINNOCK'S coolness under pressure is illustrated by this
incident, which followed his crash. The police arrived rapidly
on the scene, and for two hours he was in the company of a
polite and helpful young officer who kept calling him 'sir'.
After this spell, Kinnock, who had by now got over some of
the ghastly effect of his crash, said to the policeman: 'Look,
enough of this "sir" nonsense. My name is Neil. What's
yours?'

The young officer, slightly uncomfortable, said: 'Oliver.'

'Well, that's another fine mess you've got me into,' said
Kinnock.

IN THESE DAYS OF UNENDING political verbiage, many
people felt nostalgic about Clement Attlee, probably the
most taciturn man ever to occupy Number Ten. Colleagues of
his contributed to a pamphlet called 'Attlee As I Knew Him'.

Some people remember what a sparkling conversationalist
he was; others, like Douglas Jay, recall that 'he never used
one syllable where none would do'.

My favourite story about the laconic Attlee is related by
the former Labour Minister Roland Moyle, whose father
used to be the great man's secretary. 'A young Welsh MP,

74

Neil Kinnock & Roy Hattersley in A CHUMP at OXFORD

not without ability, but of a certain unctuousness, was summoned to Number Ten and offered a place in the government. His response at some length was to indicate that his humble abilities were scarcely, if at all, worthy of so signal an honour. "Very well," said Attlee. "Good day." The MP concerned had to wait for nearly twenty years and another leader before his chance came again.'

Lord Wilson has some good examples: Churchill often got over-excited about particular issues. Attlee remarked: 'Trouble with Winston: nails his trousers to the mast. Can't climb down.'

At a by-election in Oxford Quintin Hogg, now Lord Hailsham, was one of the candidates. He was glorying in a message of support he had received from Churchill. 'Attlee dismissed the manoeuvre with the phrase "Love me, love my Hogg".' Lord Mountbatten used to tell a story about the time he was appointed Governor Viceroy of India. After accepting the nomination Mountbatten told the Prime Minister that there was deep concern among the service chiefs that 'X' had been decided on as Chief of the (Army) General Staff. Attlee agreed: Slim was the right man. But, his Lordship pointed out, 'X' had already been told. Attlee's reply? – 'Untell him.'

THE LATE JAMES MARGACH recorded in his memoirs how Attlee's press secretary, Francis Williams, used to brief lobby correspondents about what the government was doing. Coming out of his office at Number Ten to read the test scores off the Telex Attlee asked in bafflement: 'Why is there an account of this morning's cabinet on my cricket machine?'

He never gave himself airs nor awarded himself graces, even when prime minister. At Labour Party conferences he would take a bus or tram back to his hotel at night. During elections he was not ferried about the country in an air-conditioned, video-equipped bus, nor in an executive jet. Instead his wife, a notoriously bad driver, took him from meeting to meeting. At lunchtime they would picnic on the grass verge, a perfect target for the international terrorists who in those days never seemed to pass by.

He was also notoriously mean. Once he was out at lunch with Frank Packenham, now better known as Lord Longford. Packenham was, with some justice, afraid that Attlee was thinking of sacking him from the cabinet. They ate at the Rubens Hotel in Buckingham Palace Road.

At the end of the meal Packenham, who was tired of always picking up the bill, said: 'I'm terribly sorry, Prime Minister, but I seem to have left my wallet behind. Could you possibly pay this time?'

'I'm afraid not. I seem to have done exactly the same thing,' Attlee replied.

'I'm sure they'll take a cheque,' Packenham pressed hopefully.

'Oh no, not here,' Attlee said. 'You see, they don't know my face.'

WHO IS BRITAIN'S least successful politician? My vote would certainly go to David Myles, formerly the Conservative MP for Banff.

Even at the moment of his only triumph—his election and arrival at the House—things began to go humiliatingly wrong. He called in for a drink in the Strangers' bar and an aggressive servitor behind the counter glared: 'Are you a member?' Doing his best to look dignified, the legislator pompously announced: 'I'm Myles, from Banff.' The barman shouted in reply: 'Aren't we all? I asked if you were a member.'

Lost in the maze of re-selection which followed the last constituency boundary changes, Myles pathetically toted from constituency to constituency a scrap of paper which listed all his lifetime achievements. Prominent among these was the time he had spent as 'Scout Master, Edzell Boy Scout Troop, Angus'.

No doubt impressed by these powers of leadership, the Tories in Orkney and Shetland gave him the nomination for their seat, thought to be a likely Conservative gain from the Liberals. Worse shames were to be piled upon him. The great issue in Shetland is the government's decision to derate the BP plant at Sullom Voe, which has meant that the local council received millions of pounds less per year from the company. This was all part of the Thatcherite drive to strip Britain's assets. It helped the sales of shares a treat, but in the far north the effect was described locally as 'catastrophic'.

So when they found out that Myles had actually voted for the de-rating when it came up in the Commons they were extremely angry and demanded to know the reason why. Myles's reply could have been more tactfully phrased.

'I didn't pay much attention, I'm afraid,' he said airily, 'You see I didn't know at the time that I was going to be the candidate for Orkney and Shetland.'

On election day he not only failed to register the hoped-for Tory victory, but managed to take fewer than 26 per cent of the votes.

A fascinating aspect of British politics is the way in which a man's public image can change completely, almost overnight.

TAKE DAVID STEEL. Before he became leader of the Liberal Party people assumed in an unthinking kind of way that his youthful looks and what Burns called an 'honest, sonsie face' indicated an amiable political ingenue. In other words, that Mr Steel was a nice chap who wouldn't hurt a gnat, still less a fellow member of the Liberal Party.

Then round about the time he became leader the convoluted process of changing the image began. Generally this starts when one or two journalists bother to look under the surface. Articles began to appear arguing that Mr Steel wasn't quite as nice as he looked. Sometimes he could be a tough, even ruthless, parliamentary operator. Now it is a rule that once the image has been put into reverse, it steams off with exactly the same speed in the opposite direction. So by 1983 the picture of Steel was as the Niccolo Machiavelli of British politics.

SCORES OF POLITICIANS find their images change completely over the years. Peter Walker, for instance, used to be thought of as a slippery City slicker who could be trusted no further than the length of the trajectory over which you could throw him. Now he is the social conscience of the cabinet.

ROY JENKINS'S dynamic vision and energy in the pursuit of power were going to save the country until the discovery of his lethargy let him down. David Owen was a man whose ruthless, self-obsessed ambition led him to trample over his colleagues until he became a clear-sighted articulator of the national aspirations, which he is for the time being. Of course if the SDP ever gets a real sniff of power, he will go back to being the horrid first thing.

DENIS HEALEY was just another Labour right-winger until around 1973 when the *Guardian* called him 'a thug', and a thug he has been ever since. Cyril Smith used to be a lovable jolly fat man in the public prints, though I can never understand why, since I always found him a shade morose. Then he turned into a political hatchet man before disappearing altogether. Michael Meacher, of whom perhaps 0.005 per cent of the population had heard, is becoming a swivel-eyed Leftie lunatic, though he is in fact one of the calmest, most ordinary sort of chaps you could meet.

Norman Tebbit used to be thought of as a brute and a

bully, while he is in reality a cautious politician and perfectly agreeable man. He still is thought of as a brute and a bully, but only because he wants to be. We in the press need our images; they are essential to help our poor, befuddled view of this confusing world, and we are always especially grateful when the politicians do us the courtesy of providing them for us.

NOT LONG AFTER her re-election Mrs Thatcher began a series of world tours.

I owe to a colleague this description of her visit to the Royal Dragoon Guards stationed in Germany. 'She climbed into the tank with Snoopy goggles over her red staring eyes, and charged forward, as if she was going to shout: "Let's make for the East German border, now". Her tank roared forward with clouds of blue smoke spewing out. She was hurtling over the terrain. She had bought the whole thing. Afterwards they stood and cheered her. I asked the officers if they would have cheered a Labour prime minister, and they said no, but they wouldn't have cheered any other Tory either.'

Journalists, naturally, have a collection of
weasel words just as large as politicians.

'Able': as in 'extraordinarily able mind'. Used of someone who is clever, competent but unpopular. See 'brilliant'.

'Bachelor girl': any unmarried female MP. Sometimes carries the implication that she sleeps with bachelor boy MPs, or even married ones. Sometimes doesn't.

'Bennite': used of any Labour MP who can bring himself to mention the name of Tony Benn without having to wipe spittle from his lips.

'Brilliant': used of someone who is clever, competent and also popular. Someone who bought his round in the bar last night. See 'able'.

80

'Convivial': someone who bought too many rounds in the bar last night. Synonym for 'drunk'.

'Coup': the result of being seen talking to Edward du Cann. 'In a sensational coup, Tory wets managed to get their man elected deputy vice-secretary of the prestigious back-bench paper clips committee'.

'Elder statesman': anyone who has been in parliament for ten years or more. 'Tory elder statesmen are worried that . . .' means 'the old gaffer I ran into on the terrace yesterday, chap whose name I can't quite remember . . .'

'Ferocious attack': mild criticism.

'Fiery': as in 'the fiery left-winger'. Talks too much.

'Friends': as in 'friends of Mr X warned that he would not accept the new post'. This means either 'Mr X himself, who does not wish to be seen talking to the press' or else 'some MP who once ran into Mr X in the lift and wants to exaggerate his own importance by claiming to know what he thinks'.

'Fun-loving': (male) drunk, (female) promiscuous.

'Hatchet man': John Golding MP. Alternatively, anyone who has the good sense to add up the votes on each side and so be in a position to defeat the other side.

'Hatchet job': coup (q.v.) organized by John Golding.

'Lashed out at': criticized mildly.

'Mastermind': John Golding, or anyone who uses political nous to achieve the result he wants. 'The man who masterminded the wets' control of the prestigious backbench paper clips committee . . .'

'Minder': experienced MP sent to help inexperienced by-election candidate. Carries implication that by-election candidate is an ass who could put his foot in it anytime. Probably he is.

'MPs': MP. Thus: 'Labour MPs lashed out at the stay-at-home bosses yesterday . . .' means: 'the one Labour MP I managed to contact was easily persuaded to give me a few over-excited quotes on this topic.'

'Parliamentarian': polite word for procedural bore. Anyone who can quote several pages or Erskine May and, given half a chance, will. An 'able (q.v.) parliamentarian' does little else.

'Power grab': attempt to recruit votes for vice-secretary-ship of prestigious backbench paper clips committee. Usually used after 'Bennite' (q.v.).

'Rebellion': as in 'massive rebellion'. Threat by three Tory wets that unless they get certain reassurances, they may just possibly consider abstaining on Clause 8, amendment 13 of the Paper Clips and Office Equipment (1983) Order.

'Respected': elderly, boring. 'Respected backbench MP, Sir Roger de Coverley, lashed out yesterday . . .'

'Revealed': as in: 'Secret (q.v.) documents revealed in the Daily Blast yesterday.' Used of papers which were too tedious for the other papers even to bother with.

'Row': disagreement of any kind. In the rare event of genuine emotion being felt, this is a 'massive row'. Any lesser difference of opinion is a 'major row'.

'Secret': private. Thus a 'secret' meeting is any gathering which had not been announced beforehand to the public by means of a press release.

'Secret documents': public document. Any routine piece of paper which has found its way into a journalist's hands, and is thus universally known.

'Senior ministers': code word for 'junior ministers' as in 'senior ministers claimed last night . . .'

'Sources': junior ministers.

'Split': any mild disagreement. See 'row'.

'Up and coming': 'young MP I met in the bar last night who seemed pleasant enough, though I'm blowed if I can remember his name.'

MOST POLITICIANS are suspicious of holidays because they don't like the way the country goes on happily governing itself in their absence. But nobody hates them more then the Prime Minister. Incapable of distinguishing between leisure and sloth, she makes life miserable for any of her ministers or staff who admit to the weakness of wanting a vacation.

She is as shocked to hear that they are off for a fortnight in the sun as she would be to learn that they frequented homosexual brothels. Enjoying oneself in this way is simply outside her range of experience.

One minister who had a dreadfully busy and tense 1982 (and an appalling 1983) told me how much he resented her reaction to the winter skiing holiday he had planned with his wife. 'Every bloody time I saw her she would go on and on about all the work she was going to put in during the Christmas recess. Then she'd say: 'But of course *you'll* be on holiday, won't you!' as if I was skiving off somewhere.

Another of her right-hand men confessed that he would be going off for a summer holiday. 'What on earth for?' she asked in mock amazement. 'Didn't you have a holiday at Christmas?'

A man whom I know had the misfortune to accompany her party to Switzerland. He has furnished this telling description of Mrs Thatcher's own ideal summer fun break. Largely it consists of working. No shining hour must remain unimproved. Telexes are still received, papers have to be read, new global problems mastered.

'I'll give you a typical morning,' this chap said. 'She gets up, looks out of the window at this magnificent Alpine view, and she says: "We can't climb that mountain, it's got snow on, we climbed that one yesterday and I expect there's going to be an avalanche on that one. So you'd better invite some bankers to lunch".'

CHOOSING THE NEXT LEADER makes an amusing game for Tory MPs, who spend much of their time and energy playing it. Sometimes it's known for short as the 'bus game', since the preamble goes: 'What would happen if Margaret fell under a bus tomorrow?' It is very unlikely that this will happen. For one thing, the only time she sees a bus is during the 250-yard drive from Downing Street to the Commons. Then, as Lord Carrington once said, 'the bus hasn't been built that would dare.'

AT 3.30 PM ON TUESDAY 20 SEPTEMBER 1983 a historic moment in the evolution of British politics occurred. A woman stood up at the rostrum during a session of the Liberal Assembly and demanded to know why the party's MPs were not doing more to protect gay rights. When she did so a small group of people began booing and even jeering. One shouted, 'Oh, not again'. A few moments later, Alec Carlile, the Liberal spokesman on home affairs, announced that he thought the appropriation of the word 'gay' an 'appalling misuse of the English language'. He was loudly applauded.

None of this had ever happened at a Liberal conference before. As well expect to be cheered for denouncing whales or demanding the construction of more motorways. What it goes to show is that all cases–even such mighty issues as gay rights– have only a limited shelf-life. The 1983 causes were straw and stubble-burning, female circumcision and the Carlisle to Settle railway line.

The life-cycle of a great cause is roughly this. Year One: TV documentary, probably involving Jonathan Dimbleby. Year Two: fringe meeting at Liberal Assembly. Year Three: failed attempt to get issue into Liberal manifesto. Year Four: 'massive row' at Liberal Assembly–David Steel threatens to resign unless party accepts his view that electorate will not tolerate legislation on the issue. Year Five: issue completely forgotten by Liberal Party. Year Six: it becomes official Labour policy.

NEIL KINNOCK was elected Labour leader in October 1983. I reckoned that the hard left gave their new leader a honeymoon of just 24 hours. At a meeting run by *Labour Herald*, an organ which makes *Militant* look pacifist, he was already being referred to as just 'Kinnock', a name which can be spat out with a generous spray of saliva, like 'Thatcher!' or 'Tebbit!'.

At one point the celebrated 'Red Ted' Knight, leader of Lambeth Council, said darkly, 'We'll soon put some salt on Kinnock's tail.' His new think-tank became hate figures, apparatchiks seeking power only for themselves, scapegoats for the betrayals yet to come. Ken Livingstone coined a word for the Hattersley-Kinnock leadership. He calls them 'Haddock'.

Socialist Organiser, one of the many fringe magazines of the left, published a long two-page centre-spread article about Ramsay MacDonald, to Labour folk the most hated traitor of all. The headline, in huge black type, read, 'The First Neil Kinnock'.

WINNER OF THE GERALD KAUFMAN Memorial Award for the worst dressed delegate at the 1983 Labour conference was once again Gerald Kaufman. He appeared, to the terror of passing seagulls, at first on the promenade and later in the conference hall, wearing a jacket which looked as if it had been fashioned from an Italian sofa. It was patterned in mauve, puce and green, with vivid and cunningly interlocked diamond and triangle shapes. An American colleague of mine spotted this vision coming towards him and was able to put on dark glasses in the nick of time. 'My God, he looks like the mayor of Miami Beach,' he remarked.

I WAS INTRIGUED to hear Mr Eric Heffer's explanation of why he took only 6.303 per cent of the vote in the Labour leadership election. 'The problem is that my campaign peaked too early,' he said.

THE IMMENSELY RICH Tory Treasurer, Alistair McAlpine, tells me about a folly which he has had erected near his house in Hartley Witney. It is a fifty-foot high stone column surmounted by a ball. The inscription on the pediment reads in Latin, 'This column was built with a large sum of money which would sooner or later have fallen into the hands of the Inland Revenue.'

85

The Cecil Parkinson scandal—he had made his secretary Sara Keays pregnant—burst on us in October 1983. It was one of the great British sex-and-politics stories and attracted international wonderment at our national prudery. It was also an immensely sad story.

DOWN IN BRIGHTON at their annual conference the Labour Party hardly bothered to hide its glee. In public its leading members maintained a pious silence about the Parkinson affair. In private delegates were rather less restrained. New editions of those newspapers usually described as the 'lying capitalist media' were pored over for fresh details. A true story whipped round the hall and corridors that Parkinson had been due to make a speech on the EEC entitled 'The Disadvantages of Withdrawal.' One MP asked wonderingly 'Do you think she ruffled his hair?'

The affair between Cecil Parkinson and Sara Keays began in the early 1970s after she had arrived at Westminster to work for him. She was one of scores of nice, well-bred middle-class girls who work for Tory MPs, many entirely platonically. Friends spoke very warmly of her. 'She's very nice and very pretty in a "just got off a horse" kind of way,' said one. 'She's a sort of Sloane Ranger with sex appeal.'

Curiously enough, Parkinson made hardly any attempt to hide the relationship and in some circles the two were known as a couple as early as 1976. They could sometimes be seen taking an early evening aperitif together in the Reform Club. This is not quite as odd as it seems. The various old school, regimental or clubland traditions at Westminster mean that almost no MP would ever shop a colleague over his personal life. Certainly over the years scores, and possibly hundreds of people came to know about the affair. Among the Tory MPs' secretaries it was the subject of much well-informed gossip.

The couple did appear to have been genuinely in love,

86

though Parkinson dithered endlessly about whether to leave his wife Ann and marry Sara.

In any event he didn't, so Sara took herself off to Brussels to work in Roy Jenkins's office for his last year as President of the European Commission.

Her intention was to forget Parkinson and perhaps form another relationship–friends said that he was the only real boyfriend she had ever had–but this was made difficult by his constant and urgent pleas for her to return to London. When the Jenkins job came to an end in 1981 she did exactly that and went back to work for him again.

In spring she learned she was pregnant and, so she thought, finally persuaded Parkinson to abandon his first family and make his home with her and the baby. Certainly she had no wish to bring the child up on her own however lavish the monthly cheques which might arrive. Parkinson asked to leave the break until the parliamentary recess in August when the pressure of work would be lower and a degree of discretion easier. She agreed.

By this time it was certain that Mrs Thatcher knew about the affair, though probably not about the pregnancy. Indeed, the Prime Minister is in a position to know a good deal about the sex lives of her ministers and the details are committed to confidential files. Among the principal sources are the party whips, whose job it is to keep their ears flapping for any gossip which might one day prove embarrassing to the government. As a senior Tory backbencher said: 'A chief whip must have a dirty mind.' It is inconceivable that a ten-year-affair, held almost in public, could have gone unnoticed and unrecorded.

But it is equally inconceivable that Mrs Thatcher could have sacked Parkinson because of it. For one thing, if she dismissed every minister who had been unfaithful to his wife she would have a woefully depleted government without some of its most talented members. As one senior Tory who knew about the affair for some time said: 'If she had asked him to resign it would have meant that this was the particular standard of morality which must prevail and that would have set a standard of hypocrisy which even the Conservative Party could not stomach.'

Then in late August Sara Keays had a most unpleasant shock. She was with a friend in a flat in Battersea, South London, when her door bell rang. When she opened the door an electronic flash went off in her face as a *Daily Mirror* photographer took a snatch picture. A reporter shouted at her: 'Are you going to marry Cecil Parkinson?' She slammed the door, but the *Mirror* team, in two cars, stayed ouside the flat. Some time afterwards she decided to make a break for it and, with her friend, marched out of the flat and drove off in her car. The *Mirror* men pursued them; she shook off one car, but the second stayed close. So close in fact that the cars grazed each other. Both sides blame the other for the accident.

This incident caused great alarm at the *Daily Mirror*. For some years the paper had been keeping up an image of purity and decency as part of its ferocious war with the *Sun*. Visions of full-page editorials in the *Sun* condemning their disgraceful conduct floated into haunted editorial minds. Furthermore, they had found no one who would confirm the story; there were plenty of nods and winks but no concrete evidence. They dropped the matter.

But, of course, Sara Keays wasn't to know this. She began to dread the day when the story actually appeared somewhere. According to her friends, what bothered her most was that she might be presented as a gold-digging husband-thief; a scarlet woman who had lured a rich and successful man away from his devoted family. All her friends were Conservatives; her social life centred on the party and its people, and she was terrified of becoming an outcast. She determined to make sure that when the story did emerge, it would be made quite clear that it was she who had been wronged.

Sara Keays's friends claimed that pressure was put on her to sign a statement to the effect that the whole affair had been a short, casual fling. She refused, and tough negotiations began between the two groups of lawyers. It was her solicitors who insisted on the crucial part of the Parkinson statement: 'During our relationship I told Miss Keays of my wish to marry her. Despite my having given Miss Keays that assurance, my wife . . . and I decided to stay together.'

By this time the story was out and had become the common gossip of Westminster. Even before *Private Eye* printed it the various parties were resigned to its appearance. Here there is a mystery. *Private Eye* already had a version of the story, which is not surprising since by a fortnight previously it was the common gossip of Westminster and the party conferences. They were proposing to publish a short paragraph suggesting that the Parkinson's marriage was in trouble. Then on Monday 3 October they received a long, detailed, and, as it turned out, accurate letter describing the entire affair. The letter was unsigned, and to this day the magazine's staff do not know who wrote it, though he or she clearly had an intimate knowledge of the events. Parkinson himself was partly to blame for the disclosure. He was never particularly discreet. He is, a colleague says, 'one of those people who imagine that dry white wine is a non-alcoholic drink.' He has also always had a roving eye. As he dined at the Tory conference next to an attractive if mature woman, she began to talk to him earnestly about child poverty. 'What's a pretty girl like you worrying your head about things like that?' he asked expansively.

More to the point, he was by no means as ardent an admirer of Mrs Thatcher as she of him. Possibly because he was worried about being seen as her poodle, he was happy to tell colleagues about their disagreements. He was, for example, furious about her public rebuke to Francis Pym during the election campaign.

Sara Keays finally wrecked her former lover's career the week after their affair was first made public. She was furious about the press coverage she had read. She believed that he was, by some means, getting his version of event into the newspapers. She regarded his appearance on 'Panorama' as a breach of their agreement to be silent, and she was infuriated by the suggestion—actually printed in some papers—that she had deliberately got herself pregnant.

She did not see Parkinson as a frightened, miserable figure, humiliated and half destroyed by his own foolishness. Instead she saw a man who had twice behaved disgracefully towards her and was now going to get away with it, in part by covert blackening of her name. She contacted *The Times*, hesitating only because of a laughable fear that she might upstage Mrs Thatcher's speech at the Tory Party conference.

As for Parkinson, the final verdict was unkind. When Miss Keays went to Brussels he had the chance to break the relationship cleanly, but he couldn't. In August he had the chance to break with his family, but he found he couldn't do that either. His offence seems to have been the worst in Mrs Thatcher's catalogue of sins: in the old sense of the term, Cecil Parkinson is wet.

The cruellest comment came from a long-standing political observer I know. 'The trouble with the modern Tory Party,' he said, 'is that these people regard sleeping with your secretary as a form of social climbing.'

ALL MPS' AMOURS get a lot of publicity, but cases like Parkinson's give a very misleading overall impression. I will furnish ten good reasons why MPs get their leg across rather less often than the average teacher, librarian or semi-skilled fitter.

1. Because Labour MPs live in poky south London flats which they share with other Labour MPs who have non-conformist backgrounds, who know their wives, and who snore.

2. Because Tory MPs are, by and large, rich enough to afford two full-sized homes. Therefore their Pimlico love-nest is already occupied by a wife, three children, and a much-loved labrador jokily called 'Norman'.

3. Because of the division bell. This is what Kingsley Amis used to call a 'cock-crinkler'. Imagine if, at the height of passion, you heard a bell which meant that you had eight minutes to run somewhere to save your job.

4. Constituents visiting London from northern Scotland. 'He's on the nest' is not an acceptable excuse for failing to see them.

5. Because a higher proportion of MPs than before are homosexuals, though they remain for the moment in a minority.

6. Because, owing to fire regulations, House of Commons offices do not have locks on the doors.

7. Because House of Commons secretaries are even more gossipy than MPs. Sara Keays's friends knew all about her affair with Cecil Parkinson. If you sleep with your secretary you might as well tell the Press Association immediately afterwards.

8. Because they are far too busy in boring committees, meetings, and writing letters.

9. Because Mrs Thatcher would disapprove if she found out. Being from the Welsh valleys, Mr Kinnock would disapprove even more.

10. Because if they were really interested in getting their legs over, they wouldn't be wasting their time being MPs.

OVER THE YEARS the Conservative Party conference has begun to attract as many loonies as Labour.

I went to the fringe meeting held by 'Forest', the Freedom Organization for the Right to Enjoy Smoking Tobacco. I've had a long interest in this group, largely because of their agreeably batty literature. Their general line is that it's all right to kill yourself in the name of personal liberty.

I fought my way in through a smog so thick sailors could have chewed it. There is always something faintly ridiculous about young men with pipes, and these young men had the works: pipes carved by gnomes in the Black Forest, pipes with incinerators filled with damp leaves, pipes with elaborate cooling systems like Ferrybridge power station.

The debate was kicked off by Stephen Eyres, a sort of loopy right-wing man about town. 'There is no *conclusive* evidence that one man's smoking does another man harm

...' he said, as if that made it all right. He shafted some harsh words in the direction of Sir Keith Joseph. For wrecking the health service structure perhaps? Or for building the first high-rise flats? No, for the much worse crime of 'reducing the number of smoking compartments from three in a train to two! I say this to the State!' Eyres piped, ' "Mind your own business." I say this to the anti-smoking lobby'. What he wished to say was, perhaps sadly, drowned by the cries of the audience, 'Hang em! Repatriate them!'

I surmised that as well as being keen smokers, most of his listeners were ardent drinkers too. This might account for the reception they gave to the next speaker, a cancer surgeon called David Skidmore. He was introduced as a member of the Royal College of Surgeons and the Royal College of Physicians. 'Marxists! Wets!' they yelled. Dr Skidmore said that he had in his care 800 patients with cancer. It was all very well talking about freedom, but did this mean the freedom to die of a coronary, or cancer of the bladder, at the age of forty? 'Yes, if we want to!' the libertarians screamed.

Finally Dr Skidmore, with more weary patience than I would have displayed, inquired whether, in the name of freedom, they refused to put on their airplane seat-belt when the stewardess asked them. 'I don't,' shouted the man sitting next to me. 'Didn't do Keith Wickenden any good, did it?' said someone at the back, in a tasteful reference to the former MP for Dorking who died in a light aircraft accident.

ONE OF JOHN SELWYN GUMMER'S oldest and dearest friends was telling me about his activities in the period of Ted Heath's 1970 government. Gummer was much exercised by the failings of one particular minister who he thought was out of touch with young people, resented and mistrusted by the professionals in the field, and generally ill-equipped for the job. He even announced at one point that he intended to go to Heath and request that he sack the minister in question.

John Gummer
in
HAROLD LLOYD'S
WORLD of COMEDY

Presumably and fortunately he never got round to it, because the minister was Margaret Thatcher, then Secretary of State for Education and Science.

ROY HATTERSLEY explained the style and morality of the former *Times* editor, Sir William Rees-Mogg.

Hattersley had made a number of incautious remarks about his Labour Party colleagues to a young man whom he assumed to be a member of the general public but who was in fact a reporter on *The Times*. The reporter went back to the office and wrote up his story, which duly appeared in the first edition.

When Rees-Mogg learned how the information and the quotes had been obtained he immediately ordered the story to be yanked out of all subsequent editions of that day's paper. Furthermore, since he lived near Hattersley's house in Westminster, he called round at one in the morning to apologize in person and to deliver a copy of the offending edition which Hattersley, living in central London, would not otherwise have seen. He would get, through his letter-box, a later–sanitized–edition.

At the time, Hattersley's father, Frederick, was staying with him. The old gentleman, was, not surprisingly, a little worried at seeing a perfect stranger turn up at the door in the small hours, and asked his son who it had been.

'That', said Hattersley, 'was the editor of *The Times*. He called round to give me a copy of tomorrow morning's newspaper.'

'Oh,' said his father, 'and does he do that every night?'

AS THE GOVERNMENT PURSUED its efforts to abolish the Great London Council and other metropolitan councils, the GLC's left-wingers became more and more baffling.

I have on my desk a bright and breezy monthly pamphlet (published at the expense of the ratepayers, natch) called 'GLC Women's Committee Bulletin'. It's written in clear, vigorous English, with little complicated bureaucratic phrasing and few circumlocutions. I can hardly understand the significance of one word.

For example, page 14 of one edition describes a conference entitled 'Visible Women', organized by the Women's Media Action Group. 'The morning will cover issues related to class, race, age, ablebodiedness and heterosexism,' it says. What is 'heterosexism'? Does it mean 'biased against homosexuals' as I imagine? Why should these people simply invent words and expect us to understand them? The notice concludes: 'There will be a creche on site run by Creches Against Sexism (mixed).' That last word sounds pretty otiose. You can't really imagine a creche run by Creches Against Sexism (boys only, please).

What is sad about these people is that they appear to spend much more time talking to each other than actually doing anything. There is a picture-spread in the middle of the booklet which consists entirely of photos of women talking or listening to other women speak. They were all at a meeting of the Women's Committee discussing the GLC cinema policy working party which will now look at recommendations arising from the meeting. So meetings beget meetings, reports create reports, workshops craft new workshops, liaison groups form new liaison groups, advisory panels, conferences, contracts compliance units, an endless stream of paper and talk.

Here's a snappy story headlined: 'Co-ordinating Group wants childcare and planning names!' We learn that the Co-ordinating Group liaises between the Committee Working Groups and the Women's Committee, that the childcare working group is shortly to be disbanded and re-established as an advisory group. Then, unexpectedly, 'Because Gillian Taylor has resigned as substitute for the Lesbian Co-opted Member, the Lesbian Working Group has been asked for nominations to fill this vacancy.'

One longs for an item to say: 'Fed up with the same old flower arrangements? The GLC's Floral Beauty Liaison Committee wants to hear from you . . .' Or 'Dishes to tempt

95

your hubby's jaded palate. The cookery workshop will be receiving input on cakes, pastries and jellies with man-appeal this month ...' But of course they never do. The new left isn't half as interested in ordinary people as it thinks it is.

'THATCHERISMS' became popular, and MPs began to listen for them. There was much pleasure when she was asked a parliamentary question about 10,000 CND pamphlets which Pat Arrowsmith wanted to distribute to soldiers.

'Members of the armed forces,' she replied, 'will know precisely what to do with those leaflets.'

The only person who didn't laugh at this was Mrs Thatcher herself. Opinion was later divided in the House. There were those who could not believe that it was not deliberate, and that she had simply adopted the poker face which is the mark of any truly great comedian. And there are those like me who know very well that she hadn't the faintest idea.

Remember video-nasties? For a few brief months, they were going to destroy society as we knew it.

NATURALLY MPS had a special screening and many walked out in well-publicized disgust.

Many MPs are lost, as ever, in admiration for Liberal MP Simon Hughes, the victor of Bermondsey.

The evening of the show he turned up late for the regular Liberal Party meeting. David Steel asked if he had watched the nasties, and Hughes replied, with his customary air of ponderous gravity, 'I attended only a part'.

Steel inquired whether he had been one of the members who had walked out.

'No,' said Hughes, with the same measured pomposity, 'I arrived halfway through.'

TO HOUSE OF COMMONS Committee Room Ten for the committee on the Video Recordings Bill. The seats are all taken, so in order to get in we have to idle like cars outside a busy NCP. The room is full because the MPs have turned to the question of pornography, and the seats are occupied by business gentlemen from Soho with little piggy eyes.

They sit squinting intently at the show in front of them. Occasionally they will lick dried lips, and one of them will fumble furtively in his lap, rhythmically rustling a few papers. Their steady gaze implies no pleasure in what they are watching. For them, the experience is as routine and mechanical as it is for the performers.

It is these performers who are perhaps the saddest figures of all in this dark, ill-ventilated room. Many of them arrived in London with hopes of making their fortune, or at least landing a respectable job. But as with so many of Britain's heartbreak youngsters, this proved much harder than they had thought. Faced with the prospect of a desperate struggle on the dole, they drifted into politics instead. Some, like Matthew Parris, did both.

Politics might not be 'respectable' but at least it offered easy money, comparative security, and, best of all, anonymity. Most backbench MPs are desperate to have their names concealed in case their families find out what they are doing.

Life on the circuit means they might make ten or a dozen 'speeches' (as their act is called in the jargon of this twilight world) in a single day. They will do one turn in front of the punters in the public seats, then slip unnoticed out of a side door, round to an almost identical committee room to make an almost identical speech. And if the piggy-eyed customers recognize the same rhetorical bumps and grinds time and again, their wooden faces betray no sign.

97

THE DISCUSSION OF THE BILL had, even for the House of Commons, a particularly gamey flavour. The tone was set early on by Sir Bernard Braine, the ineffable and indeed inimitable Tory MP for Castle Point, who started by being worried about pornographic computer games. I am happy to inform him that at present the state of the art would not permit the depiction of anything remotely erotic–even with the suggestively named 'user-defined graphics'.

It was Sir Bernard who initiated a lively discussion about amendment number 4: 'after "human", insert "or animal" '. He hoped to prevent cunning pornographers getting round the ban on human sexuality by showing people at it with animals. I am often struck by the way in which it is those who are most zealous to protect us from depravity who are also those most inventive in imagining what form it might take.

ISLINGTON'S LABOUR COUNCIL decided to make sure there was no racial or sexual bias in their staff recruiting.

So everyone who applied for a job with the council had to fill in a form which included this section: 'Tick whether white male/white female/black male/black female. If other, please state.'

IT IS MY THEORY that John Selwyn Gummer–by a sort of reverse Dorian Gray process–is actually growing physically younger. He seems now to have reverted to around the age of fourteen; and is telling smutty jokes behind the bike shed.

Or rather, at Scottish Young Conservative conferences. In Peebles Hydro he spent a lengthy part of his speech narrating a dirty story involving three Frenchmen and their various claims of sexual virility. I will not offend you by repeating it here, but I will point out that at seven the next morning he was up and ready to attend divine service at the local Episcopal Church.

GERRY FITT was one of the most popular MPs at Westminster and is now one of the most popular peers. He was 'introduced' into the House of Lords according to the ancient courtly ceremony. Afterwards, as is also customary, he held a party. Like all Fitt's social functions it was great fun and very boozy.

After a while, one of the country's most important heralds, the Garter King of Arms, dropped in to pay his respects to the new Lord. 'Garter', as his friends call him, was in his usual workaday rig of scarlet and gold tabard with the royal arms emblazoned on the front, knee breeches and silk stockings.

Gerry's wife Anne, now Lady Fitt, was thrilled. She turned to her husband, her eyes moist with love, and said: 'Oh Gerry, I didn't know you'd hired a band!'

SIR ALFRED SHERMAN used to be the Prime Minister's friend and favourite guru. Sir Alf took exception to remarks made by Peter Snape, the dapper legislator who serves as one of Labour's shadow transport ministers.

I fear that I cannot repeat Mr Snape's words, which might one day be the subject of legal action. But I can quote from Sir Alf's letter. This is typed (rather badly, as if by the proverbial team of monkeys which comes up with *Hamlet*) on Sir Alf's famous letterhead writing paper. This has his house number in huge letters at the top left, thus 'TEN', and the name of the street in tiny little letters next to it. It also includes his telegraphic address 'Shermania'. Quite why Sir Alf should have a telegraphic address, when there are no longer any telegrams to send to it I do not fully understand.

Sir Alf gets straight to the nub. 'You have,' he writes to Snape, 'grossly libelled and defamed me, accusing me of impropriety and bias.' He follows this with the deathless line: 'No one will impugn my integrity with impunity.'

He continues: 'I have the resources for litigation and will deploy them without hesitation to defend my honour.'

Snape is no milk-toast, to be sent whimpering away by bombastic threats. He drafted a reply telling Sir Alf that he should know that somebody else is using his notepaper. 'Obviously the man is semi-literate and appears to be somewhat unbalanced. I knew that the letter could not be genuine when I saw that the final 'c' was left off your telegraphic address.'

SEMI-SECRET SOCIETIES within the Tory Party designed to struggle against the Thatcher Terror were always fashionable. Mostly, they ate elegant dinners and drank good wine.

Few people realize that we already have a government-in-exile in Britain. It's called the 'One Nation' group of Tory MPs and its members have dinner at the House of Commons every week. It's stacked out with more dissidents than you'd find in the pages of *Encounter*. It has certainly much more talent in its ranks than, for example, the present cabinet. This is hardly surprising since a large proportion of its members were in the cabinet until Mrs Thatcher sacked them for dissidence.

The group includes Ted Heath, Francis Pym, Sir Ian Gilmour, Maurice Macmillan, David Howell, Mark Carlisle and Robert Rhodes James. Intriguingly, Richard Ryder, who used to be a Thatcher adviser (there his resemblance to Sir Alfred Sherman ends) and who married her secretary, is also a member.

There is an unwritten rule that only backbenchers may belong, though several prominent ministers retain a sort of semi-secret membership in abeyance, like Royal Masons. These include Peter Walker, Jim Prior, Douglas Hurd, William Waldegrave and, ironically, Patrick Jenkin. It was against Jenkin that so many members of the group rebelled some time ago, though I am sure there are no harsh feelings.

The group had its origins in 1951 when Iain Macleod, Robert Carr, Angus Maude and the then Lt. Col Edward Heath were members. It is unashamedly wet in its views, and

I suspect like most governments-in-exile has no real belief that it will ever supplant the usurpers in power.

It would be nice if they did. One has an image of these agreeable chaps surrounding Number Ten at dawn, seizing the chairmanship of 'Any Questions?' in a dawn swoop, lining Sir Alfred Sherman up against the wall, blindfolding him and then asking him politely to resign. But they are all far too courteous to do any such thing.

A NEW STAR emerged rapidly after the 1983 election; Edwina Currie, a Tory lady well on the way to becoming Britain's most celebrated backbencher. The publicity-crazed Mrs Currie, elected Tory MP for South Derbyshire, has had a television film about her shown on the BBC. Or rather, the film is part of a series about spouses and is chiefly concerned with her husband Ray.

He seems an affable, thoughtful kind of chap, qualities which he clearly needs. For example, on hearing that his wife blamed him for her failure to win the nomination at an earlier selection conference ('I was told he should have been looking in total admiration at my left earhole all the time I was talking,' she said), he simply took himself off to the pub.

She reveals that she vetted Ray and his family carefully before deciding to marry him. Naturally it was she who proposed to him.

Why, she is asked, does she court publicity in such a blatant manner? 'I'm quite deliberate sometimes about getting into the tabloid press and on TV because I think that if responsible politicians don't do it, then irresponsible ones will.' Hmmmmm.

Mrs Currie is sometimes described as the next Mrs Thatcher, which begs the question of whether we either need or want a next Mrs Thatcher. Certainly it is not a soubriquet she is disposed to reject. 'We do share a birthday, but that of course is pure coincidence,' she smiles, as though it could possibly be anything else.

One of her colleagues was asked the other day whether Edwina really would be the next Mrs Thatcher. 'Oh no,' he groaned, 'she's the next Jill Knight.'

In 1984 Harold Macmillan unexpectedly accepted an earldom during celebrations for his ninetieth birthday.

HAROLD MACMILLAN has never been Mrs Thatcher's warmest fan. Too many true stories indicate that. For instance, there is Ludovic Kennedy's tale about the time he went to Birch Grove to interview the old man for the BBC. At one point they set off for lunch.

'Shall we go in Mrs Thatcher?' asked Macmillan. Kennedy said he didn't see what he meant.

'We've got this new car. If you don't fasten your seat-belt, a buzzer goes off and it flashes lights at you. It's a terribly *bossy* car,' Macmillan replied.

There was the occasion when he found himself with four or five other retired prime ministers and Jim Callaghan jovially remarked that between them they could form another government.

'And we wouldn't have any women in it, would we?' said Macmillan.

Then there was the time he was to unveil a small sculpture of Mrs Thatcher at the High Temple of Toryism, the Carlton Club. Another member told me that as he shuffled towards the plinth he could be heard mumbling: 'I must remember I am unveiling a bust of Mrs Thatcher, not Mrs Thatcher's bust.'

Macmillan himself seemed on cheery form during the celebrations, though he is almost blind these days. The great birthday lunch for two hundred people was held the day after the last-but-one Soviet leader's death had been announced. Few things please old men more than hearing that they have out-lasted somebody else, and Macmillan was plainly delighted. Guests arriving at Birch Grove heard him say: 'How very considerate of Mr Andropov!'

102

Harold Macmillan
in
SUPERMAN IX

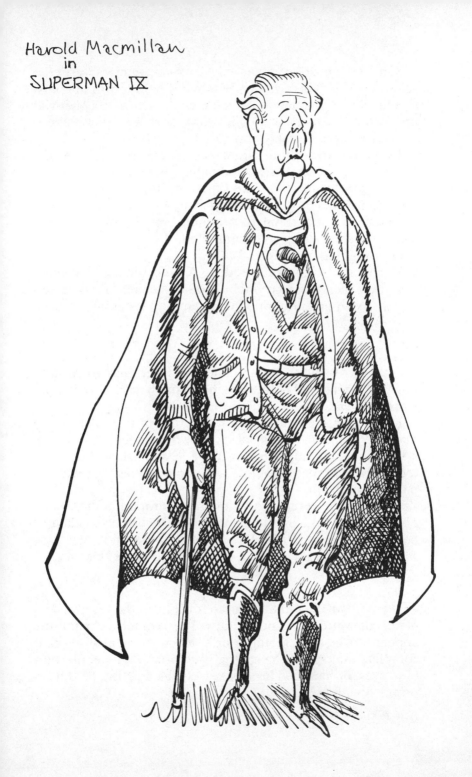

Some people noticed that only Tory ex-premiers were present, and Macmillan was asked why no Labour prime ministers had been summoned. 'Oh,' he said vaguely, 'if you invite one you have to ask them all,' which seems a tiny bit churlish, since there are only two.

I like the story about one of the speeches he gave at the Carlton Club. This was the annual Carlton lecture, an occasion of great solemnity. The time approached for the start, but there was no sign of Macmillan. An official was despatched to his room to summon him. From within the sanctum Macmillan's voice mumbled: 'I am old, I am ill, and I am not going to perform.'

Desperate action was needed. A club functionary clambered up the stairs carrying a bottle of chilled Krug champagne. At 8 pm prompt Macmillan was speaking, and on first-rate form.

AS THE YEARS WENT BY and unemployment remained stubbornly high Tory MPs found it increasingly useful to demonstrate a social conscience.

I am a considerable admirer of little Matthew Parris, the Tory MP who lived on social security for a week, to show the TV cameras it really could be done. Especially as he admitted at the end that it couldn't be done, at least not without pain and indignity.

He didn't however, fire a similar admiration in the bosom of Mrs Thatcher, for whom he used to work as an adviser before becoming an MP. 'It's absolutely typical of Matthew Parris,' she snorted. '*I* could have survived on £26 a week.'

MORE AND MORE PAPER poured forth from the GLC and its many committees and sub-groups. The Women's Committee appears to be Ken Livingstone's attempt to enrol his first complete majority. If he can only get hold of all people with blue eyes, or have two legs, or who speak English, he'll be in power for life.

Except that the Committee speaks to women in such impenetrable jargon, I doubt very much whether anyone, male or female, can understand them. Take their festivities for International Women's Day, held at County Hall London in March 1984. It doesn't sound very much fun. Like so much else which pours out of the GLC, whatever the topic, the end result is yet more talk and yet more paper.

Open day included, for black women, 'feedback and re-printed papers from the Black and Ethnic Minority Women's Conference.' Great. There was a health stall, including the Reproductive Rights Campaign, whatever that might be. There was a film show including the 'Women and Manual Trades Video, and the Women's Committee slide show about sexist advertising on London Transport.'

And so on. In their world, people aren't asked questions, but participate in 'consultative exercises'. They don't have opinions, but contribute 'feedback'. Their verbiage bears no relationship to the real language, and diminishes the several excellent causes they espouse.

Tony Benn was the Labour candidate in the Chesterfield by-election, much against Neil Kinnock's wishes. The only thing which spoiled his campaign was his victory, which made it impossible for him to blame the media for his defeat.

BENN APPEARS TO BE OBSESSED with Vincent Hanna, the portly Irishman who follows by-elections for *Newsnight* with the same unquestioning dedication that pigs follow truffles. Benn keeps trying to turn Hanna into a running joke with the electorate.

The other night he told a meeting in a school: 'We have nothing to fear, except fear itself and Vincent Hanna.' The voters tittered faintly. It's another example of Benn's failure to understand working-class people as precisely as he likes to think he does. Because *Newsnight* is broadcast to a small audience late at night on BBC2, very few know who Vincent Hanna is; if he'd said 'Robin Day', they would have known immediately.

AN INTRIGUING VIGNETTE occurred towards the end of the campaign. Hanna had gathered three visiting politicians, Messrs Heseltine, Kaufman and Penhaligon, into a makeshift studio. The idea was that they would discuss the magic of by-elections in a personal, non-partisan fashion.

Naturally this plan didn't work, and the debate soon wandered off into absurd overblown rhetoric during which Heseltine and Kaufman both contrived to blame the other's party for the rise of Hitler. (Mr Kaufman's dress sense does not, sadly, improve. When most people find their pyjamas have worn out, they give them to Oxfam. Mr Kaufman has them run up into suits.)

Another phenomenon is the manner in which politicians always accuse the press of spending a mere two or three days in a by-election town and then passing a series of instant judgements on the place and its politics. I noticed both Heseltine and Kaufman use the phrase: 'What the people of Chesterfield *really* want . . .' just 28 minutes after climbing off the train from London.

Anyhow, all this confusion may have had something to do with the interview getting off to a bad start. The lights were lit, the video cameras started turning, and the following exchange took place:

Vincent Hanna: 'Gerald Kaufman, what is so special, what is so unique about by-elections?'

Gerald Kaufman: 'You, Vincent.'

Vincent Hanna: 'CUT!'

Oddly enough Mr Benn's favourite paper during the by-election was the *Daily Telegraph* and his favourite journalist its correspondent R. Barry O'Brien. Mr O'Brien tape-recorded a lot of what Mr Benn said, and a large

106

Gerald Kaufman
in
THE COCOANUTS

proportion of it subsequently appeared in the *Daily Telegraph*, to the evident satisfaction of the candidate. Indeed, so pleased was he that on one occasion he saved Mr O'Brien's life.

They were touring the local newspaper offices, and Mr Benn was commending the example of Mr O'Brien to the neophyte hacks clustered around him. In order not to miss a single world of what Mr Benn said, Mr O'Brien walked in front of him, backwards, as if leaving the royal presence.

Unknown to him there was a long and steep set of stairs in their path. Just as Mr O'Brien was poised to disappear backwards, the candidate shouted 'Watch out, Barry!', an arm shot out, and the scribe was saved to record yet more thousands of Benn's words.

MANY PEOPLE were struck by the vivid occasion at Chesterfield when Denis Healey spoke movingly of his comradeship with Benn. 'Tony and Denis are inseparable,' he said. 'Healey without Benn would be like Torvill without Dean.' At this point, the banner of Chesterfield Labour Party fell down.

I gather Denis was less fulsome in private afterwards. 'When I say we're inseparable,' he explained, 'I mean I cannot get the bugger off my back.'

Mrs Thatcher's government does not enjoy the best of relations with civil servants.

CONSIDERABLE EMBARRASSMENT for the so-called 'first division' of civil servants during the 'day of action' over GCHQ Cheltenham. The first division are the top class, the chaps with the gold-rimmed teacups and brollies, and are not to be summoned from their posts every time some shop steward blows a whistle or waves a banner. Equally they felt a vague obligation to register some form of protest.

The horns of the dilemma were especially sharp for those at the Department of the Environment who had been working on the rate-capping bill. For the bill was to have a crucial debate in the Commons just half an hour after their strike was supposed to begin.

Finally they agreed on a compromise in the finest traditions of the British public service. When the debate began, they sat in the 'jury boxes' at the back of the Commons, reserved for members' advisers. The first time a minister requested their help, they passed him a slip of paper marked: 'Minister, we are not supposed to be here. But, if you want our advice, it is . . .' And told him all that he needed to know. Mrs Thatcher no doubt trembled at such a ruthless challenge to her authority.

A LONG AND HEATED controversy raged at the House of Commons about whether Eric Heffer is a self-centred man. This followed his denunciation as a 'personality cult' of Labour's attempts to project the image of Neil Kinnock. As so often happens in these cases, churlish observers implied that what Mr Heffer disliked was not so much the idea of a cult, but the fact that it involved the wrong personality, to wit Mr Kinnock and not Mr Heffer.

Eric finally squashed the argument by announcing bluntly: 'Well, *I* don't think I'm egotistic!'

The first real Thatcher scandal was the Oman affair. Mark Thatcher arrived in the Gulf to close a lucrative deal with the Government to which his mother had just finished talking.

PEOPLE SAID THAT BRITISH NEWSPAPERS were unkind to Mark Thatcher. To which I reply, you should have seen the Hong Kong newspapers. In particular, the *Hong Kong Standard* ran page after page about him. They called it 'an in-depth exposée of Mark Thatcher, and the companies he keeps'.

I must confess that I found it rather hard to follow, especially as most of the companies involved had surprisingly similar Chinese names. It was difficult to gasp in appalled horror at sentences such as 'Yearcom was controlled by Hon Hing Hong–a major component in Hon Hing-Trivest–and the then TBE was owned by Hon Hing Hong,' disgraceful though that might have been.

The most chilling quote came from Miss Hei Tai, a local magazine journalist who interviewed Mr Thatcher. 'He was quoted as saying his mother is perfect. "She is perfect in everything she does, whether in her capacity as a mother, a politician or simply as a human being".'

Miss Hei added, somewhat unnecessarily, that Mark was 'enthusiastic when talking about his mother, and had to be checked before he got carried away.' By men in white coats, I suppose.

MANY MEMBERS of our government began to suspect that it was being too solicitous of the various special interests.

As Norman Tebbit so elegantly phrased the problem: 'Agriculture looks after farmers, the Scottish Office looks after Scotland, the Welsh Office looks after Wales, and the Foreign Office looks after . . .' (pause for brief sneer) '. . . foreigners.'

110

Norman Tebbit
as
Will Hays
in
GOOD MORNING BOYS

The Irish problem—or, as they see it, the British problem—continued to exercise governments on both sides of the water.

UP ON A HILL overlooking Belfast is the magnificent Stormont parliament building, now the home of the fractious and much boycotted Northern Ireland Assembly. Within the vast building is the most splendid chamber of all, that once occupied by the Northern Ireland Senate.

The room is as tall as it is wide. The furnishings are all covered with thick red leather. The pillars are made from ebony, and the windows are framed with gold leaf. The walls are covered with the finest Irish damask and the fitments are made from walnut wood shipped in from all over the world. Italian marble has been used on a scale almost as lavish as that in St Peter's, Rome.

The Northern Ireland Senate has not sat since 1972, and it is almost inconceivable that it will ever meet again. As Shelley might have written (but didn't) of its only memorial, 'Look on my works, ye Catholics, and despair.'

A MEMBER of the Dublin parliament, Niall Andrews, objected to the decision to extradite the suspected terrorist Dominic McGlinchey. McGlinchey should not be sent North, Mr Andrews explained, because he would not get a fair trial there. Instead he should be locked into a Southern jail and the key thrown away.

IN SPITE OF ITS HUGE MAJORITY the government became obsessed by the prevention of Parliamentary rebellions. A Tory MP told me about the extraordinary pressure which had been brought to bear on him by the whips when he decided to vote against Mr Jenkin's bill to abolish metropolitan council elections. Since only 19 MPs planned to do the same, and since the government still had a majority of 93, you might imagine that ministers would not be too bothered. Bothered, however, they were.

'It was like one of those films about interrogators,' he said. 'One of the whips was the kindly, civilized chap who brings you the cup of coffee and a cigarette. He just said: 'Are you going to be silly on Wednesday?' The other was the brutal one, you know, the one that slams you in the stomach. He yelled and shouted and called me a "stupid****"

'They aren't remotely subtle about it. I had endless interviews, there were endless attempts to make me change my mind. They don't mind using the crudest type of blackmail. One of them said: "You do realize that this means the end of your political career." '

None of this had any effect, and my chum voted against the bill anyway. No doubt it will bring his career to a temporary halt. But not, I suspect, for more than a few years.

I WAS CHATTING to a Tory MP about Mrs Thatcher's fifth anniversary, and her evident determination to stand for a third term of office. He sounded gloomy.

'As Lord Carrington once remarked after a cabinet meeting,' he said, 'what can you do with a woman who you can't make love to and you can't make laugh?'

'Did Lord Carrington really say that?' I asked.

'No,' he said, 'I did. But it sounds so much more convincing if Lord Carrington said it.'

BY 1984 Ken Livingstone had become a figure popular enough to merit a best-selling biography, by John Carvel.

Carvel went to south London to interview Ethel Livingstone, Ken's mother. He had been told earlier that both parents were Conservatives.

'I believe you were both Tories,' he said to Mrs L.

'No dear,' she said. 'I'm Taurus, but his dad was a Leo.'

113

MRS THATCHER'S successful deal with the Chinese over the future of Hong Kong did not come all that easily. The problem is that the Orientals find our Ministers all too scrutable. Take, for example, Mrs Thatcher's visit to China a year or so back. She had been told that Clare Hollingworth was the acknowledged British expert on Chinese minds, tiny or otherwise. The British embassy in Peking arranged for the two women to meet in Hong Kong so that the Prime Minister could receive an expert briefing.

Mrs T. swept into the room.

'My dear,' she announced, 'I believe you are the doyenne of China correspondents. Now the problem as I see it is like this. . . .' There followed a two-hour Thatcher discourse, during which time Miss Hollingworth was not able to utter a single complete sentence. At the end of the session she was so angry that she remarked, simply but eloquently, 'Thank you for seeking my advice, Prime Minister,' turned on her heel and walked out.

None of this did Mrs Thatcher much good. On leaving the Great Hall of the People, she stumbled and fell on the steps. The Chinese are superstitious and took this as an exceedingly ill omen.

During her interview with Chairman Deng (or T'iang, or Dung–you know who I mean) she fiddled nervously with her jewellery the whole time. This might not matter, except that the Chinese greatly dislike personal adornment, and regard it as doubly rude to call attention to it. As Ms Hollingworth vividly put it later: 'It is like farting in front of the Queen.'

*There was some heated controversy when a
Tory MP was arrested by plain-clothes police
in a gay club.*

THE NEWS about the entrapment of MPs recalled an unfortunate mishap which occurred to Mr Elwyn Jones, now Lord
Elwyn-Jones, and our former Lord Chancellor.

He was representing a chap in one of those public lavatory
cases, this one involving the Gents in Piccadilly Circus. The
case turned on the evidence of a young plain-clothes constable, so Jones thought it would be a good idea if he and his
junior visited the Gents in order, as it were, to reconstruct
the offence. Most sensible people, I should point out, would
rather risk a hernia than enter this appalling establishment.

Jones and the young barrister were deploying themselves,
one at a stall, the other advancing towards him, and Jones
was the while giving the other instructions. At which point
another constable laid hands on both their shoulders and
said, 'Right, I'm having you both.'

'But you don't understand, I'm a barrister!' the QC
exclaimed.

'Ho yes, we get a lot of barristers in here,' riposted the PC.

'But I am Elwyn Jones, QC,' said Elwyn Jones, QC.

'Pull the other one,' said the policeman.

This all could have gone on forever, but happily Jones had
on him his pink-ribboned brief (as opposed to pink-ribboned
briefs) and was able to secure release for himself and his
junior.

TIME TO PRAISE Nicholas Soames, Tory MP for Crawley,
and a fellow once universally decried as the King Of The Parliamentary Wallies. People disliked him for his rude and
boorish manners and his greedy appetite. They felt that he
made his father, Lord (Bunter) Soames, appear like a svelte
and elegant faun.

One day Nicholas swung up to Dennis Skinner, the

Robespierre of the Labour Party, the sea-green incorruptible Member for Bolsover, who will not accept a cup of tea from somebody if he suspects that a Conservative might once have glanced at the empty pot.

'Look here, Skinner,' Soames shouted, 'I'm coming up to Derbyshire this weekend for some shooting–with Andrew Devonshire' (a reference to the Duke of Devonshire, who is master of Chatsworth House and a stupendously rich landowner).

'I thought I might look in on you,' he continued. 'So, will you do it properly–lay in some gulls' eggs, that kind of thing, and get that wife of yours out of her curlers. All right?'

It is a tribute to Skinner, who lives in a small terraced house in Clay Cross, that, instead of setting a hundred flying pickets on the saucy Tory, he took the joke quite well and sat silent with a glassy grin.

Soames was playing in a cricket match for the Commons XI, captained as ever by Colonel Michael Mates, Tory MP for Hampshire East. Mates is a man I would follow anywhere–into the jungle or the lounge bar–but his wicketkeeping that day was not of the finest. Indeed he had let no fewer than forty byes past his gloves when he suddenly barked to the team, 'Come on now! Pull yourselves together!'

At this point Soames rolled up to him and announced: 'You have been sitting there all afternoon looking like a tart in Montmartre. You have more holes in you than a second-hand landing net, and you are telling *us* to pull ourselves together.' The colonel was silenced thereafter.

A CURIOUS FOOTNOTE to Denis Healey's most famous remark. You may recall that some time ago the Shadow Foreign Secretary addressed a sixth form conference at the Central Hall, Westminster. After the usual series of reverential questions had been asked–how should we approach the Common Agricultural Policy, what is your attitude to

116

Hong Kong, and so forth–a youth stood up and boldly demanded: 'How bit is your plonker?'

When Mr Healey replied brusquely, 'Big enough,' he was cheered loudly. It seemed a remarkably quick and quashing riposte, and gained a lot of publicity.

I now learn from Chris Price, the former MP who chaired the meeting that Healey did not actually hear the question at all. He asked Price to tell him, and the chairman, who had also misheard, said, 'He asked, "How big is your conker?"–he must mean your head, I suppose.'

For much of the parliament it was assumed that the next Tory leadership election would be between Norman Tebbit and Michael Heseltine.

TEBBIT WAS INTERVIEWED on TV-am about another of those leaked documents which pour out of ministries as fast as the photocopiers can print them. As usual when he is in an uncomfy foxhole, Norman attacked the interviewer, accused various people of thieving the documents, and generally created a good, soupy, acrimonious atmosphere.

After the spot was over, he was shown to his car by Clive Jones, the boss of TV-am. As they walked out Mr Jones was startled to see the Secretary of State patting his pockets in some annoyance. He inquired what the matter was.

'Oh nothing,' snorted Norman, 'I was just making sure that you hadn't stolen my wallet as well.'

TEBBIT WAS IN ACTION at the Portsmouth by-election in 1984. I liked his definition of the difference between a moderate socialist and an extreme socialist. 'An extreme socialist is one who wants to abolish the public schools tomorrow. A

117

moderate socialist wants to abolish them after his children have finished going there.'

MEANWHILE HIS MAIN RIVAL, Mr Heseltine, had been trying to establish himself as one of the lads, an ordinary chap like you or me. A friend of mine who is also a journalist was called in, with a small group of other hacks, to see him in his office for a briefing. The weather outside was particularly bad, and my friend was wearing gumboots. When he saw the thick, lushly woven Axminster carpet on the ministerial floor he felt rather ashamed of these and asked Heseltine if it would be all right for him to step inside.

'Of course!' he said warmly. 'I have a pair of wellington boots myself. But I keep mine at my *country* house. How clever of you to keep yours in town!'

I FOUND MYSELF in Brixton, south London, some time ago. It proved a strange, slightly disquieting experience. For Brixton, as well as being the scene of some of the worst riots in 1981, is also the centre of Lambeth, the borough presided over by ungenial, unsmiling 'Red Ted' Knight.

It seems a very bossy place. People are always telling you what to do and what to think. Outside the Tube station a group of youths were brandishing copies of *Socialist Worker* and instructing travellers to 'smash the Thatcher regime'. On the steps of the Town Hall, known locally or at least to local papers, not always the same thing) as 'Red Ted's Castle', three more youthful persons with loud-hailers were telling the populace to back the miners.

As one of them droned on about the evil Thatcher-MacGregor axis, the others advanced on shoppers with collecting tins. The shoppers used their marginal vision to veer quickly out of their way, like people faced with life insurance salesmen.

Everywhere in the borough there were posters. Some

were merely curt: '*Don't* Jump The Lights.' Others used the ratepapers' money to solicit support for the preservation of the GLC–a cause which I myself support, though I am mildly annoyed to find my own money being spent to tell me I do. Others, plastered all over the Town Hall and various nearby sites, attempted a forced jocularity, like a schoolmaster who imagines that his bullying can be made tolerable through heavy jollity.

'Are you a racist? You'd be so much nicer if you weren't,' says one. I'm never quite certain what the definition of a racist is, but I feel pretty certain that whoever these people are, they won't be moved by that poster.

The whole district has a feel of permanent revolution about it. One imagines spontaneous self-criticism sessions taking place near the Tesco check-out, public trials in the recreation ground, row after row of posters on the public buildings instructing you in every aspect of correct thinking.

Happily, most of the citizens I saw were ignoring it all in a resentful sort of way, rather as people living near Heathrow ignore the planes. It is one of the greatest strengths of our small nation that most people are so uninterested in politics.

I HEAR of a very cunning wheeze. Sir George Young, a minister of notably wet views on social issues, had his phone number printed by the racist and neo-fascist rag, *Bulldog*, with an encouragement to its loony readers to ring him up and give him their views. This is what they did, sometimes at three in the morning.

Sir George then hit upon a splendid idea. Every time the phone rang during the day, he or his wife sent their five-year-old daughter to answer it. After a few moments, even the racist morons realized that she couldn't understand any of what they were frothing about.

'But she learned an awful lot of new words,' her father tells me proudly.

IN IRELAND I learned about the bizarre and clandestine visit of the Rev. Ian Paisley, who arrived in Dublin at the dead of night in order to fly-post various government offices. He was objecting to the report of the 'New Ireland Forum', a document prepared by various nationalist political parties, and in Paisley's view, up to no good.

Indeed, it is in itself startling that the Reverend Doctor should deign to descend to the South for any reason. God, for example, would not demean himself by trying to stick up fly posters in Hell.

Things went badly wrong from the start. A guide whom Dr Paisley had engaged to point out to him the various administrative buildings was caught by the police driving in the wrong direction on a one-way street, and so the turbulent cleric had to find his own way about. Finally he worked out where the Prime Minister's offices were, and set to work gumming up his posters. At this point, two policemen (or *'gardia'* in Irish) passed on patrol. One of them shone a torch in the miscreant's face. 'Why, it's yourself, so,' he said to Dr Paisley. Paisley agreed that it was and promptly, my informant tells me, 'fekked off back to Belfast'.

Denis Thatcher doesn't always receive the same amount of press coverage as his wife does:

WHEN THE PRIME MINISTER last visited Canada, her consort walked down the back of the plane for a chat with the journalists, or 'reptiles' as he does sometimes call them.

'Do you know what Canada is full of?' he enquired. 'Canada is full of fuck-all.'

After a few more similarly genial remarks, he returned to his seat. Later a somewhat nervous functionary from the Number Ten press office came down the back. 'Did Mr Thatcher have, er, much to say?' he asked.

The Rev.
Ian Paisley
as
Andy Devine
in
STAGECOACH

'Yes,' the hacks told him. 'He said that Canada was full of fuck-all.'

The functionary blenched and blanched at the same time, then dashed back to the front of the plane. Mr Thatcher did not speak to the press again during the trip.

WHEN HE ACCOMPANIED his wife on her tour of China, he spent seven days there. Then he got on to the plane to come home. One of the journalists covering the trip asked him what he thought of China. He pondered a moment.

'China is full of fuck-all,' he said, adding: 'I don't mind if I never see it again.'

The hack asked him: 'What is your favourite place in all the world, Mr Thatcher?'

This time he thought a while longer, and finally announced: 'Dallas'. I expect he thinks J.R.'s problem is that he's too soft.

MR THATCHER is fond of repeating the fact that his wife turned down the pay rise she could have had in order to set a good example to the rest of the nation. Indeed, one of his choicest themes is the huge cost to the Thatcher purse of their selfless service to the nation.

But he does have one consolation. The money received by retired prime ministers is pegged to the amount which goes to the current occupant of Downing Street. 'At least it means that Ted doesn't get his extra pension!' Mr Thatcher chortles, often.

BBC employees pass round among themselves a home-made tape of Great Moments in Radio, some of which never actually got broadcast.

THE SECOND ITEM on the tape features our Prime Minister and offers a splendid opportunity for me to welcome back Gordon Reece, her personal image maker, from his long exile in California. Mr Reece has returned as a sort of executive garbage man: it will be his job to sweep the banana skins into the gutter before the black patent leather shoe skids on them.

Back in 1979, though, he was still in England and teaching his pupil, the leader of the Opposition, how to address her future subjects. If the tape is anything to go by, she was a slow but, by golly, a determined learner.

She begins her address to the nation thus: 'If, as I hope, the minority parties join with us next Wednesday, we shall not only be able to set the wheels in motion, we shall also have re-asserted the historic right of the House of Commons to say to the government of the day "enough is enough".'

This is where the trouble begins. Mr Reece interjects with a low, polite mumble, then advises: '*Enough* is enough. A lowering, not a raising.'

Before he has finished, she chips in again. 'Enough is *enough*,' she says. 'No-o-o-o,' Mr Reece muses. 'ENOUGH is enough,' she tries again.

Mr Reece, like a modern Henry Higgins, shouts cheerily, 'That's it!' But nothing will stop her now. '*Enough* is enough. Enough is enough. Enough is enough. Enough is enough.' As if about to join her in song, Mr Reece chants with her in unison one refreshing burst of ENOUGH is ENOUGH.

Four times more she says it, each time in subtly different fashion. There is the boldly assertive: Enough is enough! The faintly interrogative: Enough is enough? The soft, pliant: enough is enough. The stern and resolute: Enough Is Enough, no doubt as used against the Argies.

'Right!' says Mr Reece happily, innocently thinking that might stem the tide. But nothing will–the voice continues, rising, plangent and plunging, and the tape fades out as the phrase is again and again repeated, like a Hindu mantra, vested with a spiritual meaning which most of us can only dimly discern.

A CURIOUS NEW PHENOMENON in British politics is the arrival of the 'minder'. The word is somewhat misused; in the TV programme it refers to an, admittedly lovable, hired thug. Politically the term means the brains of the outfit.

A minder has the job of looking after an inexperienced by-election candidate and preventing him or her from making too many stupid mistakes. Most candidates have a lot to learn. They have to be told not to make rash promises, not to get involved in doorstep rows, not to harangue the press and never to admit that there is a possibility of losing.

They don't always succeed. In my experience, candidates with minders generally lose, though this may well be because if they were good candidates they wouldn't need minders in the first place. Jim Lester MP was the minder for the Tory candidate in Chesterfield, who came third. The winner was Tony Benn, who didn't have a minder.

Neither did Roy Jenkins, who beat the Labour candidate in Hillhead. He was a left-wing social worker who wore an ear-ring, and so required the services of Donald Dewar MP as minder. Michael Mates MP, the former army officer whom one would follow into the jungle or a cocktail lounge, minded for the Tory at Portsmouth South, where the Conservative suffered an unexpected defeat.

I don't suppose this last surprise had anything to do with Col. Mates's robust campaigning style.

'Of course,' he would boom, 'this is the dirty end of the constituency . . . ah, good morning sir, would you care to meet our candidate?'

One house had the name 'Hoggart' written up by the doorbell. 'Hoggart, eh!' he bellowed genially, 'that's a pretty silly

124

name if you ask me.' Fortunately for the Tory candidate, Mr Hoggart (no relation) was not at home, and so missed the colonel's droll animadversions on our nomenclature. Apart from this, Mates played a blinder, and it wasn't his fault that Mrs Thatcher is now so frightfully unpopular with the voters.

Minders are inclined to chip in at press conferences. 'I think what Nick is trying to convey here is that . . .' On the doorstep they subtly take over the conversation. 'Hello Mrs, er, Smith, I'd like you to meet the Labour candidate in this election, Reg Pargiter. I hope you'll be voting for Reg on Thursday.'

Mrs Smith mutters something vague.

'Now, are there any questions you'd like to ask Reg, because he's here now, meeting you?'

Mrs Smith inquires, for example, when the council are going to unblock the estate's drains.

'Right, yes, that's a real problem. But you know, Reg can't do anything about your drains unless you elect him on Thursday. So, help to get him into parliament where he'll really represent your interests, all right, Mrs Smith?'

Throughout this monologue, Reg has stood around looking vaguely foolish, or patting the Smith dog in an effort to find something for his hands to do. By this time the minder is on his way to the next house, gabbling the while to passing journalists to make sure that it is him they listen to, and not any more of Reg's silly gaffes.

NICHOLAS SOAMES, portly, offensive, much-loved Boy Bunter of the Conservative Party, was promoted to glory–to wit, became parliamentary private secretary to the tiny John Selwyn Gummer, chairman of the party.

This is, of course, bizarre. It is as if a school fag had been made head boy and the captain of cricket obliged to rush about polishing shoes and toasting crumpets. Gummer is small, eager, perpetually boyish. Soames is vast and majestic. He is also the grandson of Winston Churchill. Those who see them together gaze first at the boss, then at the underling, and finally walk off somewhere dark, to work it all out quietly in their minds.

WHEN YOU THINK of the great political phrases and phrase makers—'fight, fight and fight again to save the party that we love'; 'Most of our people have never had it so good'; 'Lower than vermin' and 'Some chicken, some neck' for example—it seems sad that rhetoric is now a dying and possibly a dead art. Insecure, unsure of their nostrums, fearful of the electorate, modern politicans seem to prefer verbose waffle to elegance and wit.

The arrival of the Alliance brought with it an even more turgid style, which I think of as uniquely SDP-ese. It is the language of the computer instruction manual, of people who are accustomed to thinking not about the real world but in terms of breeze-block concepts pushed together to make serviceable but ugly constructions. David Owen's book, a collection of his speeches and articles is, I regret to say, almost entirely written in this fashion.

Take this clause, typical of the section on prices and incomes: 'Disaggregation of national wage-bargaining procedures will only help if there is a decentralized employing authority . . .' Try embroidering that on your banner.

Dr Max Atkinson, an Oxford don, wrote a brilliant analysis of the rhetorical devices used by politicians in his book Our Masters' Voices.

THE TRICKS are not too complicated: always let your audience know when you expect them to applaud, by gesture, intonation or sentence structure; make good use of contrast

126

('They are the party of the easy option; we are the party of reality') and say everything in threes: ('United in purpose, strategy and resolve'; 'Friends, Romans, countrymen'). Dr Atkinson makes a special study of Tony Benn, who he says makes in one year more speeches than some of the most famous orators of classical Greece made in their lifetimes.

Benn's cleverest knack, he reveals, is to speak *through* the applause. Though he makes sure that nothing of his argument is lost, his voice chopping through the claps has several effects: it makes him appear modest (ignoring the enthusiasm of his supporters); it implies that his message is so important that it cannot wait for the clapping to stop; and by cutting the applause short, it pens up the excitement, so that at the end of his speech, the audience finally erupts in unbounded acclaim. Dr Atkinson points out that John Kennedy used much the same technique.

One intriguing point which he doesn't mention (strictly, I suppose, it's outside his topic) is this: the most popular speakers very often have a speech defect or peculiarity. This works, I think, because sitting listening to somebody talk is basically a most tedious activity. Some curiosity of speech helps to focus our attention and prevent it from straying.

Benn, for instance, combines a silibant *s* with a not very successful proletarianism: 'Yer know, zhozhializhm izhn't juzht about zhpending money.' The content of a Roy Jenkins speech isn't all that gripping–it's mostly long abstractions– but delivered with the famous lisp and the unique hand gestures it commandeers the attention. 'An entil-y weasonable weadiness to come to terms with wationality,' blended with the famous hand movement in which he cups a firm young breast, is irresistible.

For many people accents are their greatest advantage. Neil Kinnock brilliantly uses his Welsh, as Nye Bevan did before him. David Steel fails to cash in on his soft Scottish accent, which is why his platform oratory is so much less effective than his persuasive TV manner. The best Commons speaker I ever saw, Brian Walden, had both trouble

128

with his *r*s and a fascinating Black Country accent, slightly less pronounced than Powell's. Norman Tebbit has a strikingly flat London accent.

Margaret Thatcher is not a natural orator, and I suspect she would sound better if she had kept the Lincolnshire accent she must once have had. Michael Heseltine has no regional accent, but uses another device: he always begins as the epitome of calm, then after about twenty minutes appears to go completely berserk, as if the monstrosities of socialism had driven him to the edge of his reason.

EDWINA CURRIE, the publicity-crazed Tory MP for South Derbyshire grew so annoyed at the way that the 'Cross-bencher' column in the *Sunday Express* persistently called her 'publicity-crazed' that she contacted the journalist—to offer him an interview.

I ALWAYS LOVE THE Liberal Assembly. For one thing, they go in for immensely long resolutions. Whereas the Tories favour three-line jobs ('affirm our faith in Prime Minister's leadership . . . call for tougher action against hooliganism . . . etc), the Liberals debated a motion on the Place of Women which was 85 lines long—more than 750 words. The complexities were far too much for the delegates to unravel. At one point, the chairwoman announced triumphantly: 'Before you vote on "either" or "or", you're going to be voting on "and"!' as if that made it all clear.

EVERYONE EXCEPT THE FAR LEFT was frightfully cutting about Eric Heffer's chairmanship of the 1984 conference. Eric's seat in Liverpool is not entirely safe from the Militant Tendency (remember that these people thought Stalin right-wing) and so he called an enormous number of Trotskyites from Liverpool to speak. Mr Kinnock even made a joke about it at the conference revue: 'Eric has pledged his

129

support to four key areas in the fight for local democracy. They are north Liverpool, east Liverpool. . .'

But then Eric has always had trouble in converting his emotional spasms into action. There was the incident when the party's national executive held a meeting at the House of Commons rather than in its usual room in Labour headquarters. At one point the argument became heated, and Eric declared: 'I'm getting out.' With which he stalked off and flung open a door which turned out to be a cupboard. So he marched next door, which was also a cupboard. He flung open a third, and a couple of brooms fell out. 'Oh, sod it, I might as well stay' he muttered, and sat down.

The Tories' most momentous and tragic party conference took place in Brighton in 1984. It began cheerfully enough.

EVERYONE AT BRIGHTON was craning their heads, hoping for a glimpse of the lovely, intelligent, publicity-crazed Edwina Currie, Tory MP for South Derbyshire. It had not actually been a very good month for Edwina, who hoped to be appointed to one of the three places vacant in the whips' office, and thus clamber onto the fluffy-covered footstool of power. The word is that the Prime Minister, having been one of Edwina's greatest admirers, has now changed her mind and has decided not to advance her career yet.

Edwina first burst onto the gaze of the astonished world when she addressed the 1981 Conservative conference on the topic of law and order. At one point, in order to illustrate her argument, she produced a pair of handcuffs and waved them from the rostrum. La Pasionara of punishment. Among those watching with slack jaw and bulging eyes was Lord 'Grey' Gowrie, now the only poet in the Cabinet. 'Oh

130

God,' groaned Gowrie as he stared at Edwina, 'I feel the bat squeak of desire.'

The same event had a different effect on Lord Whitelaw, who was then Home Secretary and was obliged to reply to the debate. 'I spotted her as a wrong'un some time ago,' he said later. His problem was that Edwina sat on a parole board for which he was responsible. Her fellow members were so upset by the handcuff-brandishing incident that they requested Willie to dismiss her.

Now, of course, no Tory home secretary can sack somebody merely for being a success at a Tory party conference. 'So I did what I always do in such situations–nothing,' said Willie.

THE ROLE OF RESIDENT SPECTRE at the conference used to be filled by Ted Heath, though people don't seem to notice him so much these days. He has certainly lost none of his gossamer sense of humour. At a reception he marched straight up to Lord (David) Young, who had just been appointed to the cabinet with the job of stirring up British industry.

Heath announced: 'I used to think you were intelligent. But you've taken a job where you'll have no influence in cabinet, without a political base in Whitehall and with no chance of achieving anything at all. As I say, I thought you were intelligent–that is, when I found out who you were'.

Was it a joke? Heath's friends say it was, but then it must be extremely hard to tell the difference.

DURING THE CONFERENCE I went to the Dome Theatre in Brighton to attend a concert John Wells had arranged to mark his new book *Fifty Glorious Years*, a mock tribute to Mrs Thatcher and, especially, to her husband Denis. Wells appeared in the military costume of a Ruritanian prince consort, and acted as MC for a series of short musical items.

Every time one sees his performance one believes that it

131

cannot be lifelike; the real Denis cannot be such a caricature. Then you hear of a genuine conversational snatch.

While Wells was depicting him on stage, Denis was having a drink half a mile away, and talking about left-wing infiltration of our broadcasting services.

'When Margaret wants to know what's on the BBC, I don't tell her, instead I say "It's on Mafia"–you know, as in Marxist Mafia 1 and Marxist Mafia 2.'

TORIES LOVE BUYING things. Among the objets achetés available at Brighton were marzipan busts of Mrs Thatcher, four inches tall, guaranteed to last six months and costing only £2.50. Who could actually put such a thing in his mouth? You'd feel like a pervert. One of the nastiest things I saw was a large red sticker marked 'Cancelled due to lack of public support'. This was for gumming over posters which advertise events organized by your political opponents.

Without any doubt the single most devastating event so far in the whole of Mrs Thatcher's government was the bomb which exploded in the Grand Hotel, Brighton, a few minutes before 3 am on Friday 12 October 1984.

THE NOISE OF THE EXPLOSION was so great that for an instant it seemed to have disconnected the senses. Nothing could possibly be so loud; it could not be real; it must be some appalling hallucination. This trance-like state continued for a few moments more, since the noise–a rumbling, earthshaking thunder then a tremendous splitting crack–was followed by an equally unexpected silence.

In the street outside the Grand Hotel nobody moved and

132

nobody made any sound. The handful of people nearby were silent, apparently frozen where they were standing. Then, terribly slowly, the thick grey cloud of dust and smoke billowed out from the hotel towards the sea.

The policemen outside suddenly recovered themselves and started to shuffle the mesh barriers to block the roadway. The first arrival on the scene was a drunk who kept insisting on trying to walk through, until they had to shove him out of the way. Perhaps he had not even heard the noise, since the report made by a bomb travels in a peculiar, unpredictable way, sounding quite different even to people who are near one another when it explodes. Several guests in the hotel actually slept through it and had to be woken and told to get out.

This sense of a mingled dream and nightmare continued in the street immediately afterwards. There was Sir Keith Joseph, splendid in silk pyjamas and dressing gown, sitting bewildered on his official red box of government papers, which he had clutched to him as if it contained his family jewels. There were small knots of people, the survivors of the Grand's bar and lobbies, covered with the choking grey dust which shone luminously in the TV lights. 'His last words to me were "we *must* do something to stimulate the economy," and whoosh. I thought, "My God" . . .'

Not everyone was in nightclothes; some had not gone to bed, and others had found time to dress. A minister and his wife had dressed neatly, almost formally, as if going to a first night. They moved briskly about, the British middle class refusing to be flapped, looking for ways they could help. Then an hour later I saw the wife quietly sobbing on a couch.

Roy Bradford, who served in several perilous Northern Ireland governments, was a few feet away from the explosion and was saved by a couple of walls. He and his wife had thought that day of switching to a room with a sea view; the room no longer exists. Neither of them had ever been so close to a bomb in Ulster.

The refugees from the Grand crossed to the Metropole, and were then ejected by another bomb scare. But when it

133

re-opened they served coffee to the evacuees and even opened the bar, so that a bizarre social event followed, a sort of pyjama party mingled grotesquely with the fear of what might be found under the rubble next door. There were plenty of jokes; people kept saying that it was like the blitz, and so it was, though the blitz passed in an upper-class bomb shelter, perhaps a basement nightclub in Mayfair rather than a tube station. Men and women in evening dress drank brandy and laughed in a faintly hysterical manner.

I wondered why people felt, sporadically, so light-hearted. Part of it must have been relief, of course; it hadn't happened to them, just as hearing the crack of a rifle tells you that the bullet has not hit you, since it would arrive before its sound. Principally it was because we didn't yet know that anyone was dead. This bubble-headed feeling did not last for long.

Someone would be anxiously asking where was their friend X, surely he had been staying in the Grand, was it really true that Y had told Z he had seen him near the station? Then as dawn appeared, quickly, almost furtively, through the corridors, the lounges and out on the shingle beach, were whispered the names of those who were thought to be missing or dead in the wet and stinking rubble. Some of the names were true.

'I do hope The Speech is uninjured,' someone asked. Sir Alfred Sherman, who used to be one of the Prime Minister's advisers, politely offered emergency help with The Speech, her final address to the conference. The offer was declined with equal courtesy by Gordon Reece, who still is one of her principal advisers.

Throughout the week of the party conference Mrs Thatcher keeps The Speech on the boil, like some terrible peasant stew, feeding it each night with more words tossed in by her writers and aides. On the Tuesday night The Speech had been torn up and thrown away ready for a fresh start on Wednesday. It had finally been completed just a few minutes before the bomb exploded.

In a curious way, until the Friday Mrs Thatcher seemed

134

distanced from the conference, as if she was not really present. She didn't come to many debates, and missed Norman Tebbit's speech as well as Michael Heseltine's. (She usually skips Heseltine, though in 1983 she did turn up and shortened his standing ovation by sitting down first; he was quite pleased she didn't come last year.) Her first public speech was a short but baffling address at the Young Conservative Ball just before the traditional dance with the YC chairman and several dozen jostling photographers, unaccountably to the tune of 'The Lady is a Tramp'.

In 1984 she told the sweaty revellers, 'There must be no weakness. We must stand together,' then perhaps realizing this hadn't entirely caught the disco fever mood, distractedly added: 'Tonight you can dance together. Tomorrow, you must stand together.' For a chilly moment she evoked a world in which life is nothing but confrontation, relieved only by an occasional song from Duran Duran.

The column visited the USSR with Neil Kinnock and Denis Healey.

THE LAUNCH SITES for SS-20 missiles (the ones which are pointed at us) are not included on the tourist itinerary for visiting Western politicians. This is a pity, since some of them are reckoned to be no more than a day trip from Moscow. If Mr Kinnock and Mr Healey had gone to one instead of to the Summer Palace, they would have found a group of nine flat-bed wheeled trucks, each with a 49-foot rocket on its back. At a time of great international tension, these trucks will be driven out through miles of thick forest along roads which probably don't appear on any map.

When the thing is launched at us, it will stop climbing somewhere over Germany. Then the three warheads will separate and fall towards different cities or bases. If you happen to be standing on one of these spots and look up, the

135

last thing you will see is a silver cone-shaped object, a little like a sawn-off ice cream, tumbling down towards you.

During Mr Kinnock's talk with Mr Chernenko, the Russian leader said that if Britain removed all nuclear weapons from its soil, 'the Soviet Union would guarantee that its nuclear weapons will not be trained on British territory'. This sounds like splendid news, though some people did wonder how long, in the heat of a crisis, it would take the Russians to train them right back again.

And it would take quite a while. *Jane's Weapon Systems* says that a slight direction change of one or two degrees could be managed in seconds, but 'if the targets are widely separated it might require 20 or 30 minutes for re-targeting'.

Well, that's a start. Mr Kinnock's trip at least might have bought us all an extra twenty or thirty minutes before we are turned into our constituent molecules. Years ago there was a grim parlour game in which people asked how you would spend the four-minute warning. Now, thanks to the Labour mission, we can get something useful done—finally putting up that bathroom shelf, perhaps.

I don't mention these morbid details to detract from the success of the trip. It was not as it happens a diplomatic triumph, since there was no real negotiation. On the other hand, the Russians saw the meeting as a useful means of sending all sorts of encouraging messages to the West. Mr Healey spent most of his time showing off, as is his habit. Spotting the greeting party at Moscow airpirt, he said cheerfully, 'Same old Mafia, I see'. In the fabulous Hermitage museum in Leningrad he was unstoppable. We collected his most plonking remarks. 'You know whoever he was painting, Rembrandt really painted himself,' he averred. 'That Van Gogh looks just like a Gaugin. Of course they lived together at the time. . . .'

The most annoying thing about Mr Healey, though, is that he actually does know his stuff. The proportion of bullshit, I would guess, is under thirty per cent. This makes him a very useful chap to have around in such a baffling place as the Soviet Union.

136

He thought this had been much the most productive and good-natured of all his six trips (though it couldn't have been worse than his first, in 1959, when the party spent all but half a day sightseeing, Harold Macmillan called an election, and Hugh Gaitskell got so drunk–or conceivably, drugged–that Nye Bevan had to hold the press conference). The group met Boris Ponomarev six times. At 79 Ponomarev is one of the very few survivors of the Stalin period to remain both important and alive, and he clearly took a shine to the Labour delegation–he even tickled Mrs Kinnock's hand when he took his farewell, an experience she found somewhat disconcerting.

He also described her as 'the most beautiful woman I have ever met', which may be true. Later he sent her a set of his collected works–in Russian. She hasn't yet read them.

A MEASURE OF THE SOVIET DESIRE to improve relations was the warm welcome given to the Kinnock delegation. As a special treat, the hacks accompanying him were allowed to visit the Holy of all Holies–Lenin's apartment in the Kremlin. Here, in this obscure flat set into the Council of Ministers' building, was Lenin's study, Lenin's bedroom (like the Duke of Edinburgh, he slept apart from his wife), Lenin's library–with his own, well-thumbed copy of *Das Kapital*–his phone, his pen, and even his blotting pad with the mirror-image text of his last letter faintly visible. The guide explained his many saintly qualities: his capacity for ceaseless hard work, the six languages he spoke fluently, his ability to read 600 pages of books each day, his brilliance at science. A conducted tour of the carpenter's shop in Nazareth would be less reverent.

Then we passed down a short corridor, and there it was: an ordinary sort of board room, not especially large, with a long rectangular table lined with simple chairs: the room where the Politburo had met from 1918 to 1958. This was where all those dark and terrible events were plotted and where some of them took place; here was Uncle Joe's chair from which he glowered down the table at those who had not

137

much time to live. There were portraits on the wall—not his, nor Leon Trotsky's, but their ghosts were present.

THE CULT DOES REACH absurd levels. Some time ago the Soviets produced a book about the young Lenin, designed to impress good behaviour on small children (indeed the small children in a school we visited all wore the inevitable red and gilt badges—showing Lenin as a child of four).

The book is full of exemplary tales about how the little Vladimir Ilyich never answered back, always worked hard, was polite to grown-ups, and so forth. The book was a great success in the Soviet Union, and so the government decided to reprint it in other East European languages. Here it did less well, except, puzzlingly enough, in its Polish edition. They could not get the copies out fast enough.

It then turned out that Polish students were holding riotous parties at which the highlight was readings from the book. These would be declaimed in a suitably heroic manner. 'And before Vladimir Ilyich went to bed he always brushed his teeth, making sure that he brushed his gums as well and not forgetting the teeth at the back. . . .' The book was immediately withdrawn from sale.

As the Soviet Union tried to recreate its links with the West, Russian officials made approaches to surprising Western politicians:

THEY HAVE BEEN TRYING for ages to get Ken Livingstone, leader of the GLC and thus spokesman for nine million oppressed Londoners. Ken, however, is no lover of the Soviet system, whatever the *Daily Mail* might think, and has so far resisted their offers. They are getting desperate. One day a functionary from the Soviet embassy pleaded with him: 'But Mr Livingstone, you promised you would come over and visit our Jewish dissidents.'

138

THERE ARE TWO KINDS of politician. Those who are 'one of the lads' and those who aren't. To put it at greater length, there are those who try to convey the impression that they are mere members of the public who happen to have taken up legislating as a career, instead of mining or chartered accountancy. On the other hand, there are those who wish to appear set apart from the rest of us, elevated perhaps, maybe even predestined to lead.

Naturally the categories can get confused. Harold Wilson tried to be one of the lads, whereas in fact he was a clever statistician with a First from Oxford. James Callaghan attempted to be a leader set above us, whereas he was really Stoker Jim, one of the boys from below the decks.

Mrs Thatcher is not one of the lads, though Norman Tebbit is. Willie Whitelaw is one of the lads too, for this is not a class-based thing. Lord Soames was a lad in his day, though Lord Home would not know what the term meant. Michael Heseltine is not a lad, nor is Sir Keith Joseph. Mr Biffen is most certainly one of the lads, though perhaps the shy one who has to be persuaded into joining in the pub sing-song.

Mr Kinnock is as much one of the lads as it is possible to be. Mr Kaufman is not. John Smith is; Peter Shore isn't. Dr David Owen isn't either, though I have my doubts about David Steel. He has certain laddish qualities, though I feel that he dresses a trifle too neatly.

Roy Jenkins wouldn't know what a lad was if you brought one to him in a wickerwork wine basket. Shirley Williams is a lad (the term is uni-sexual; after all, 'one of the lasses' sounds twee rather than comradely). Tony Benn is a non-lad posing as a lad, whereas Arthur Scargill is the genuine article.

How do lads behave? You may tell them because they are more relaxed in private; they might drink a little more than is good for them, and even use the kind of language you would not expect to hear in a political speech. Approach them privately after a party meeting to ask them what transpired and they will tell you that it was bloody awful. Make

140

the same inquiry of a non-lad and he will gaze at you glassily before vouchsafing: 'The party is in excellent heart.' Non-lads are always on duty.

Put a lad down on a train and he will take out the latest Dick Francis. The non-lad sitting opposite will have the abstract of European pig-iron statistics or *A Future That Will Work* by David Owen. On the rare occasions when lads produce books, they tend to be collections of risqué anecdotes compiled for charity. Non-lads write great abstract works with titles like *The Centre Cannot Hold*, or *Nexus-Led Society*.

Lads always keep in touch with their local football teams and claim to be able to get you tickets for Wembley (which they never can). Non-lads have scant awareness of anything outside their own small world, and ask questions like: 'Who *is* Boy George?' Forced to recognize that there is a life outside politics, they preface remarks thus: 'My children tell me. . . .'

When a lad starts a speech to his constituents, he opens with a breezy anecdote (no doubt culled from his own compendium) and claims that it actually happened to him. The non-lad begins: 'Ladies and gentlemen. Our nation faces a crisis as great as any in its history. . . .' When a lad is demoted, or his party is defeated in the election, he says: 'Win some, lose some.' The non-lad regards it as a crushing blow, and one which may place the nation in mortal danger. Non-lads have a solid appreciation of their own importance.

They are often conscious of their non-ladlike qualities and try to set the image right. Non-lad chancellors of the exchequer are always photographed on the Saturday before the budget, playing on the lawn with their children and the family dog–but always looking as if they have just been introduced. Lads go for the statesmanlike visionary, Karsh of Edmonton look.

If they have love affairs, lads tend to be fairly open about it and get caught out. Cecil Parkinson was, perhaps, the ultimate lad.

MRS THATCHER really did see the miners' strike as her personal war effort into which the whole country should throw its endeavours.

She was chairing Cabinet Committee 101, the group which included the ministers involved in the strike. Somebody pointed out that the Nottinghamshire miners, the ones who had been working throughout the dispute, were due to begin their annual holidays.

'Oh, but they can't do that,' the Prime Minister exclaimed. 'You must tell them, they mustn't go, they've got to stay at work. We need them.'

It was the Chancellor of the Exchequer, Nigel Lawson, who had to point out gently that the Notts miners were working not for the greater glory of the government, but precisely in order that they could enjoy such luxuries as annual holidays.

SURPRISINGLY, Arthur Scargill is a secret admirer of Mrs Thatcher. This goes some way to explaining why the miners' strike lasted such a very long time.

A friend of mine who works in television was chatting to Scargill at a studio in London. The conversation turned to the Prime Minister. 'You know,' said Scargill, 'she and I are very much alike. We say what we mean and we are determined to get what we want.'

In other words, the rest of us were caught in between two stubborn, pig-headed people. Do you think that she admires him as much as he admires her? I rather doubt it.

THE MINERS' STRIKE was not noted for clarity and plain speaking, so I was particularly pleased to see this thoughtful aperçu from Moss Evans, general secretary of the TGWU, whose union gave £30,000 to the miners. 'Money is not everything,' Moss mused, 'but it does make poverty tolerable.

142

Arthur Scargill
in
MUTINY ON THE BOUNTY

POLITICIANS do enjoy each other's funerals, and lots of ours have had plenty of fun lately going to the frequent obsequies in Moscow. In most cases they only see their Soviet counterparts when they are already boxed-up, as indeed happened with Mr Chernenko. Indeed Mr Kinnock, the sole member of the British party to have met the dear departed at length, was presumably the only one suffering from a sense of personal loss.

David Steel and David Owen had encountered him much more briefly, at Mr Andropov's funeral. Owen peered at Chernenko closely and concluded—using his expertise as a doctor—that he was suffering from emphysema and did not have long to live.

When the wacky pair returned some months later to see Chernenko himself lowered into the ground, the lid of the coffin was removed and all the world statesmen were asked to file past the embalmed figure of the late general secretary. As the Alliance leaders walked by they looked in. 'Well, he certainly looks a *lot* better now, doesn't he?' Steel remarked loudly, to Owen's vigorous assent.

Yet more examples of the Prime Minister's strange behaviour have been logged:

NEIL KINNOCK visited her at her rooms in the Commons to discuss the names of Britain's next EEC commissioners. 'Ah, good morning, Mr Kinnock,' she said. 'Would you like some coffee?'

Her guest explained that though he liked coffee, he had drunk quite a lot that morning and didn't want any more.

'But I insist. You *must* have some coffee.'

'I don't want any, thank you, Prime Minister.'

'You must have a cup of coffee.'

This went on for quite some time until finally he won, and

had a short, caffeine-free meeting. 'I could only imagine that she simply could not have her will thwarted in anything, even over a cup of coffee,' he says. 'It certainly wasn't that she wanted me to enjoy her hospitality. She simply had to win, and only gave up when she realized how absurd the whole thing was.'

AT CHRISTMAS 1984 Mrs Thatcher ran a celebrated girdle round the earth:

The Prime Minister's extraordinary journey around the world appears to have had the one purpose of demonstrating her tremendous stamina. It doesn't seem to have achieved much else. President Reagan, having been brought up in the Middle West in the early part of this century, finds it very difficult to disagree with a woman. She bustles in, wags a metaphorical finger at him rather like a small-town school-marm, and he smiles and says: 'Why, yes.' Meanwhile the hard-faced men behind him get on with whatever they were planning to do in the first place.

But her stamina was undoubted–though it was presumably helped by the fact that, alone on the plane, she and Sir Geoffrey Howe had proper beds to sleep in. The trip was five and a half days long, and the party was in the air for an average of ten hours a day. On Friday 21 December they took off from Hong Kong in the morning and flew for twenty-four hours, stopping off briefly at Guam and on Hawaii. They finally arrived in Washington in the afternoon of that same 21 December–with more work to do. Back home it was the shortest day of the year. For the Thatcher party it was, literally, the longest day of their lives.

The hacks accompanying the party did not survive anything like as well as their Führerin. As days merged into nights and one world capital blurred into another, they found that they were being put to bed at two or three in the morning and woken up an hour or so later. In Hong Kong they were told to be up with their bags packed at 5 am in order to attend her press conference, scheduled just before

145

her departure to Washington. They refused, saying they knew perfectly well every detail of her views on all the topics which might be covered. They were firmly told they would have to come and that there would be no alternative transport.

So they went, but under protest, and sat at the back refusing to ask any questions. This exposed Mrs Thatcher to the pitiless interrogation of the Hong Kong reporters, who asked all sorts of rude and difficult questions for the whole period of the press conference. The Prime Minister's staff sat glowering at the British hacks, who smiled sweetly and silently back at them.

CAREFUL RESEARCH into John Selwyn Gummer's past revealed that he has been creating embuggerances for years. Back in the past decade when Gummer wore a sort of Arctic explorer beard and looked much older than he does now, he worked for the British Printing Corporation as an executive. One of his jobs was helping out with National Noddy Week, seven days of festivities to commemorate the tiny wimp with the bell on his hat. Gummer had to order some 10,000 Noddy badges, for distribution to small children.

Unfortunately, owing to a slip of the brain he added two extra noughts and ordered one million of the things. They still sit in sacks, clogging up corridors and cupboards, a clinking memorial to Gummer's enterprise.

146

POOR, DEAR EDWINA CURRIE is still having difficulty ingratiating herself with her fellow Conservative MPs. It is with great regret that I report another churlish insult to the lovely member for South Derbyshire, this time coined by Nicholas Fairbairn. He, you may remember, had an unfortunate relationship with his secretary, who tried to hang herself outside his house. It was known at the time as The Case of the Swinging Secretary.

The debate was on fluoridation of our water supplies. Mrs Currie supports it, and Mr Fairbairn doesn't, on the grounds that too much of anything is poisonous. 'Were we to spreadeagle Mr Fairbairn on the floor of the House and pour absolutely pure H_2O into him, it would kill him in hours.'

Fairburn was instantly on his feet. 'All the poison that my honourable friend suggested I would happily take, rather than be spreadeagled on the floor of the House by her.'

Try saying it in Fairbairn's croaky voice, like a wounded capercaillie.

Incidentally, Edwina baffled another of her colleagues on the first day she arrived at the House. She was queuing to sign in, as all members must after each election, when she turned to the chap next to her and said: 'Please excuse my accent– I'm trying to learn Derbyshire.'

He tells me that from that day to this he still hasn't worked out what she can have meant.

MUCH DISTRESS among the Commons hacks when Sam, the hyper-efficient barman, went off to work for the Conservative Party. He ran into Neil Kinnock at a party in Westminster. 'Sam,' said Kinnock, 'why are you going to them? Why didn't you come to us?'

'Because the Labour Party didn't have a vacancy,' he replied.

'Oh Sam', said Kinnock, 'the Labour Party is one big vacancy.'

IS TONY BENN all right? I mean, really really quite *all right?* A friend who works for BBC radio tells me of the strange experience which befell one of their most distinguished reporters. He was sent round to Holland Park to interview Benn about a notorious left-wing demonstration in the Commons.

When he arrived with his tape-recorder, Benn answered the door carrying *his* tape-recorder, and, what's more, brandished the microphone in the poor fellow's face. As the reporter stammered out the various courtesies—good of you to give me an interview, weather a little warmer now—Benn walked in front of him, backwards, the microphone always at mouth level. Benn even negotiated the steps down to the basement floor backwards with hand mike aloft.

The interview proper then began. The reporter (John Sergeant, one of the best known and most experienced at Westminster) asked Benn about Mr Kinnock's strictures on the left's behaviour. After one question he asked another on the same topic. Benn suddenly snapped into his 'the-BBC-is-an-enemy-of-the-people' mode, accusing all BBC employees of being agents of the Thatcher Government.

Sergeant said that there seemed little point in an interview which did not discuss the party leader's reaction to this well-publicized incident, and said that the matter might be resolved by discussion with his editor, who was in Broadcasting House.

While he was being put through to her, to suggest that she had a word with Benn, he turned round to see that the MP was holding over the BBC tape-recorder a gadget called a de-magnetizer. This is an electro-magnetic coil available from any hi-fi shop, which wipes recording tape clear instantly. So the whole interview so far was destroyed.

According to my BBC chum Sergeant was so angry and offended by this that he tottered straight out of Benn's house, feeling, no doubt, a little like Jonathan Harker finally quitting his host's Transylvanian castle.

148

Eric Heffer & Tony Benn
in
HORSE FEATHERS

UNLIKE OURS, American election campaigns begin immediately after the previous one has ended. I met Senator Gary Hart at a working breakfast. Hart is that unusual phenomenon in America: the party politician. Most presidential candidates regard the party as a handy vehicle for their ambition, whereas Hart, I think, believes that the Democratic Party actually has a soul of its own.

He has also mastered the British technique of knifing your opponents while appearing to slap them on the back. He was particularly lethal with Senator Edward Kennedy, who might be one of his main rivals for the Democratic nomination in 1988.

'Teddy Kennedy is a very good friend of mine. We sit next to each other in the Senate. You know, he called me up during the primaries last year and asked me "what are these new ideas?"'

'Is he one of the old, discredited generation of Democrats? Well, that's for others to say, not me,' he beamed, implying that is precisely what he meant. Later someone asked him why he thought Kennedy had made his terrible visit to South Africa. Was it because he genuinely hated apartheid? 'Well,' said Hart, 'we can start with the first possibility–that he meant what he said.'

The suggestion that the truth was merely one of several options open to Senator Kennedy was masterly. Perhaps Hart is not the David Owen of American politics, but the Norman Tebbit.

I RAN INTO A TORY MP who was scurrying off to take part in the debate on corporal punishment. He was not looking forward to it. He told me: 'You can always tell when a politician is lying: when he says, "I'm glad you asked me that question," "It's time to get back to basic principles; or "It's corporal punishment which made me the man I am today."'

UNLIKE THE REST OF US, politicians hear a kind of instant reply of their own words, inside their heads, every time they speak in public. This wish to pre-censor anything which might cause them subsequent embarrassment can lead to some strange effusions.

Sir Gerard Vaughan, who sounds more like the hero of a period romance than the Tory MP for Reading and former Health Minister which is what he actually is, has produced a sex education video for use in schools and youth organizations. The video makes it clear that sex before marriage is right out. Shouldn't happen, jolly dangerous, leads to pregnancy, VD and general moral turpitude.

A somewhat surprised reporter from *The Times* phoned Vaughan and pointed out that he had not married until he was 32. Had he himself abstained from sex in all his years between adolescence and wedlock?

'I can't remember,' said Vaughan. The reporter said she was startled by this. It did seem the kind of thing that was rather difficult to forget.

'Well, all right,' said Vaughan, 'the answer is yes and no.'

The reporter, even more baffled, suggested that in such matters there could hardly be any yes and no about it.

'Oh yes there is!' said Vaughan triumphantly, closing the conversation.

What can he have meant? The mind is thrown into turmoil by such a reply, which is perhaps why *The Times* decided to spare its readers the details of this exchange.

A GAME down at the Commons is twisting MPs' names to fit well-known proverbs or sayings. Two of the first: 'Flannery will get you nowhere,' (how true) and 'He who Heseltines is lost' (even truer).

Later suggestions from readers included: 'Hayhoe, Hayhoe, it's out of work we go,' from the name of Treasury Minister Barney Hayho; 'The Winterton of our discontent'; 'Once Brittan, twice shy,' and my favourite: 'There's nowt so queer as Fookes.'

151

THE TV SHOW 'Spitting Image' led to a new social phenomenon at Westminster. Far from being insulted by their appearance, the more self-important MPs became offended because they weren't singled out.

How can any politician have street credibility with his own teenage children if there isn't a hideous, wart-festooned latex model of his face in Limehouse? One man who I hope will receive the accolade soon is my old friend Eric Heffer. It would be a fitting climax to his years of public service.

I reject absolutely the opinion of one of Heffer's colleagues: 'The trouble is, if they did a puppet of Eric, it would be so much more flattering than the real thing.'

The Defence Secretary began to behave in a curious manner. He affected military dress, and refused for quite some time to explain why. Finally he had to say something.

AT LAST we had an explanation for Michael Heseltine's decision to wear a camouflage combat jacket during the heroic clearance of women from the Molesworth Peace Camp. Mr Heseltine says that, although he had planned the whole operation with great care, he had forgotten to take a coat, and it was raining. Presumably he borrowed the gear from a passing officer, or Millets.

I would certainly not venture to disagree with the Defence Secretary; apart from anything else, I cannot afford the secretarial costs. However, as I recall, the weather in England at that time was seasonal, and most chaps were no more likely to leave behind their coats than their shoes.

SOON AFTERWARDS Mr Heseltine invited in for drinks journalists who had accompanied him and Mrs Thatcher on

Michael Heseltine
in
WORZEL GUMMIDGE

their visit to Washington. The hacks were astonished to hear him talking about the Clearance of Molesworth as if it had been an epic military victory, on a par with Agincourt, or Goose Green. At first they assumed that he was joking, but as he hammered on about what a brilliant success it had been, how meticulously planned, how superbly executed, they realized to their horror that he was entirely serious.

Heseltine even boasted about how plans for the operation—which involved the expulsion of a bunch of unarmed pacifists, mainly female—had been told to soldiers only in tight little groups to minimize leaks.

'He was completely carried away,' said someone who had been standing there with his jaw slack. 'He seemed to have lost any touch with reality.'

A NAME which may, one day, be as hideously familiar to Mr Heseltine as those of Clive Ponting and Tam Dalyell is that of Derek Hanlin, an otherwise unknown gentleman who lives in Porth, Glamorgan. Mr Hanlin has taken it upon himself to extract from the Ministry of Defence the whole truth about the Defence Secretary's brief military career.

Mr Hanlin has sent an awful lot of letters to the MoD and has received quite a few replies. What is startling is the slowness with which the information was released to him—just a little extra smidgeon of fact each time.

For instance, the first reply (from Major P. Westrope, Retd.) merely confirmed that Heseltine had served as an officer in the Welsh Guards during his national service. The next letter reveals the titbit that Heseltine, having joined the ranks earlier in 1959, was an officer for a mere two months, from July to September. Major Westrope added: 'He resigned his commission when elected as an MP.'

Mr Hanlin points out that Heseltine was *not* elected in 1959; indeed didn't make it to Parliament until 1966. What he had in 1959 was the Tory nomination for Gower, a safe Labour seat. Mr Hanlin wonders whether he had the nomination all stitched up before he accepted the commission–knowing that a political candidate could not continue to serve in HM Forces.

Major Westrope's next letter confirms this rule, adding that the soon-to-be-Tarzan had quit under paragraph 672 of the Queen's Regulations. Even this turns out to have changed since.

Mr Hanlin now has quite an impressive historical dossier, no doubt for use against the day when Michael Heseltine becomes Leader of the Conservative Party. I cannot quote all of it, since some of his points may be libellous, but he does find it curious–to say the least–that the Defence Secretary appears to have been the first person to have used the paragraph 672 loophole to get himself out of national service after such a short time.

Of course, Mr Hanlin adds drily, the paragraph was drafted at a time when officers were also gentlemen. So, I suppose, were Defence Ministers, then.

The Environment Minister, Sir George Young, reported another Tony Benn sighting.

SIR GEORGE was travelling back one Saturday from the Midlands, where he had attended a conference. The only other passenger in his first-class compartment (MPs go first, at our expense) was Mr Benn, who was travelling back from his constituency, Chesterfield. Though it was a non-smoking compartment, he was puffing on a pipe. Now and again people–chiefly young–would recognize the celebrated polemicist and chat to him. He replied courteously and at length.

In between times, the minister tells me, Benn listened to one of those Walkman personal tape recorders. The sound of voices leaked out of the foam earpieces, and the minister inquired whether Mr Benn was listening to opera. But no, it turned out that he was not listening to music at all but playing through tapes of *his own speeches*, and continued to do so all the way to St Pancras.

155

BENN HIMSELF described another incident which occurred while he was on a train. A thuggish looking young fellow walked down the aisle and stopped at his seat.

'Here,' he said, 'you're Tony Benn, aren't you!'

Benn acknowledged that he was.

'You're a Conservative, aren't you!' the youth continued.

'Excuse me,' Benn inquired, 'but are you a *Sun* reader?'

'Bloody hell, how did you know?' the boy asked him.

A popular topic for discussion was the name
of the rudest MP at Westminster. In the end,
the decision was not too hard.

SO, STEP FORWARD, the Emperor of Insult, the Nabob of the Nasties, Douglas Hogg. Mr Hogg is the Tory MP for Grantham and the son of Quintin Hogg who–rumour has it–still stalks the cabinet room, moaning gently and rattling his chains.

Until 1984 Hogg was a government whip, a job which he did incredibly badly. Whips have to know instinctively when to be sharp and when to mollify or appease. Hogg was just lacerating all the time–not only to other young snapper-whippers like himself, but to the distinguished old jossers as well. For example, he once barked at Sir William Clark, a former Conservative deputy chairman, 'The Tory Party may have made you a knight. But it has not made you a gentleman'.

Hogg is a whip no longer. He resigned, amid a great deal of relief on all sides. His role had been as absurd as having W. C. Fields in charge of the Woodcraft Folk. Now, he is enormously happy, and once again gleefully carols each joysome morning.

There was the celebrated occasion when an East Midlands MP–among his duties Hogg had the task of shepherding the Tories from this area–decided not to vote with the leadership in a division on local government. He had mistakenly

156

failed to notify Hogg of this fact. At 9.40 pm, just twenty minutes before the vote was due to take place, Hogg stalked into the chamber in order to berate the recalcitrant MP. As the minister at the dispatch box droned on with whatever collection of flannel and half-truths had been strung together by his civil servants, the voice of Hogg could be heard, higher and higher, angrier and angrier.

At this point, Sir Anthony Kershaw MC, one of the most distinguished and respected MPs in the party, came over to Hogg and requested him to desist. Hogg swung round and shouted at him: 'Go away and get a cup of black coffee.'

Sir Anthony, a man noted for his sobriety, was furious.

AN INFORMANT TELLS ME of the rudest remark he has heard of even Hogg making. There is a body called the Blue Chip Group of Conservative MPs, most of whom are patrician, landed wets of the type Mrs Thatcher is alleged to despise, but whom she nevertheless keeps popping into government jobs. They dine together now and again, to discuss the dreadful failures of government policy and the difficulty of finding decent factors and pig wormers for their substantial farms.

Some time ago the group produced a booklet, written by the Hon William Waldegrave MP, which argued that the Prime Minister was on the wrong course, ought to change her mind, more jobs, waste of a nation's future and so forth. The booklet caused quite a stir at the time, and among those who complained most stridently was the right-wing MP for Orpington, a barrister called Ivor Stanbrook. He said, among other things, that the tome had been produced by a bunch of wealthy layabouts, most of whom had never done a day's work in their lives.

This is the small change of abuse at Westminster, and Tristan Garel-Jones (Watford)—one of the people whose name was on the book—was chatting quite amiably to Stanbrook in the members' lobby shortly afterwards. At which point, up stalked Hogg, who brusquely interrupted the conversation, pointedly inserted himself between the two men, turned to Garel-Jones and said: 'I would have been proud to have put my name to that pamphlet. You should completely ignore Stanbrook. "Never done a day's work, indeed! Why, there is not a solicitor in the country who would *give* Stanbrook a day's work!"

With which he stormed off. It is, of course, always possible that he did not recognize Stanbrook's face. But I doubt it. Hogg is made of a firmer fibre than that.

MRS THATCHER made another gruelling tour of the Far East, a locality where she spent far more time than in the north of England. The tour, during which she compared British workers to 'children', also brought her a new nickname to add to her collection.

The 'Empress of India' was adding to our store of harmless fun with more of her surprising remarks. It was an eventful tour.

In Jakarta the hotel where the hacks and minor officials were staying appeared to be infested with deaf-and-dumb prostitutes. It was thought lucky, in view of their handicap, that Denis Thatcher was staying with his garrulous wife at a government guest house—otherwise he might have been sorely tempted.

Trying out a British-built electric bus on rails in Malaya Mrs Thatcher asked for reassurance: 'It will take us gradually round the bend, won't it?' Not gradually enough, I fear.

Most typical was her remark to Lee Kwan Yu, the Prime Minister of Singapore. When he asked why she had not brought a doctor on such an arduous tour, she said: 'If I had brought a doctor, *I* would have had to look after *him*.'

THE PROSECUTION of Clive Ponting did not deter the moles in the Ministry of Defence. An executive officer—who justly wishes to remain anonymous—sent me a letter listing the various nicknames used at the MoD for his boss—Michael

158

Heseltine. My informant tells me that the one name he is never called is 'Tarzan'–like 'the Beast of Bolsover' for Dennis Skinner, that particular term is employed only by the popular press.

He is variously referred to as 'Blondie', 'Goldilocks', 'Frankenstein', 'Maggie's Darling', 'Maggie's Boy', 'He Who Must Be Obeyed', 'Maggie's Golden-Hearted Treasure' and, by certain younger members of his private office, 'Er Indoors.

In May 1985, the launching of a new group to deflect the Prime Minister from her chosen course didn't go off quite as well as its organizers had hoped.

THE LAUNCH of the Centre Forward group, Mr Francis Pym's alleged shock force, was certainly not handled well. But, on the other hand, I don't think it was quite so much of a disaster as the jubilant Tory leadership seemed to think at the time.

For a start, there was Mr Geoffrey Rippon's grumpy TV interview the day after Pym's Oxford appearance during which Rippon said how much he disliked the speech and complained how nobody had asked *him* what ought to be in it.

Now Rippon was something of a surprise choice for the steering committee, not least because he is really rather right-wing and not at all in sympathy with most of the group. He also spends quite a lot of time making money in the City instead of beavering away in Parliament. It is, furthermore, suspected that his real objection to Mrs Thatcher is the fact that she passed him over for ministerial office.

In any case, his dissatisfaction with the group caused them no distress at all. Indeed, they had proposed to sack him from the steering committee, and so his threat to resign merely relieved them of a certain embarrassment.

Ted Heath was not invited to join, on the excellent grounds that if he had agreed to he would have done the new group more harm than good. The Heath Group in the Conservative Party has at the moment only one member, to wit, E. Heath (Con., Old Bexley and Sidcup), and his appearance in Centre Forward would, I regret to say, have allowed the Thatcher people to write it off altogether.

Nevertheless, Heath can't be expected to see things that way, and was tremendously hurt. A super-duper high-level delegation, consisting of F. Pym and Sir I. Gilmour, was despatched to calm him down, which it barely succeeded in doing.

There was one fascinating mystery. Plans for the preparation of the group took some weeks, and were conducted in as clandestine a fashion as possible. As the day for the public launching neared, Pym announced that he felt it his duty to tell the Chief Whip, John Wakeham. This is the way things are done according to the form of the Tory Party.

Pym's colleagues did not want him to go. They felt they needed the extra time, and asked Pym, just for once, to forget he was a gentleman. Pym is no more likely to forget that fact than he is to forget his trousers, so off he went regardless to see Wakeham.

When he told him about the group, Wakeham smiled broadly and told him that he had known all about it all the time; indeed a mole (or, as we used to call them, an *agent provocateur*) had attended every planning meeting and had sent the Whips a full report.

'But I haven't told anybody,' Wakeham added with a grin.

Did he mean he hadn't told the Prime Minister? It very much sounded as if he hadn't. I wonder what she would have to say about that.

The public relations man for the new group was Julian Critchley, who had recently published an admirable book in which he complained gently that he had failed ever to become a minister. One of his colleagues in Centre Forward consoled him. 'At least you've got a job now, Julian,' he said. 'Aide-de-camp to the Grand Old Duke of York.'